Mentally Ill

Or
Frustrated & Unhappy?

By

Michael Rice, LISAC, CTRTC

Mentally Ill
Or
Frustrated & Unhappy?

ISBN-13:

978-1983849930

ISBN-10:

1983849936

Edited by Lynn Zacny Busby

Madeira Publishing
1550 E. University Drive, Suite J-1
Mesa, AZ 85203
(480) 898-3015

Table of Contents

Introducing Dr. William Glasser

When I began a new career in my late forties, I had just enough knowledge to know enough to tread lightly, and cause no more harm to any of my clients. I had yet to develop the skills I felt I needed to be an effective therapist. After four years of relying on the psycho/social concepts of Erik Erikson's developmental psychology, I found it to be too involved and time consuming to deal with many of my client's needs in the area of substance abuse and relationship problems.

Not being satisfied with my results, I began to utilize the principles of Albert Ellis and Rational Emotive therapy. I found this to be somewhat more effective than what I had been relying upon, but still I was not fully satisfied. I felt there had to be a more efficient form of treatment that could be easily understood and explained to my clients that would give them insight into taking charge and empowering their lives.

It was my introduction to Glasser's Choice Theory that had a profound influence not only on the lives of my clients, but in my own personal life as well. Dr. Glasser came upon the scene in the 1960s and his approach was controversial over other modalities that many leading professionals and professors considered his concepts to be naive and was omitted in many of the university text books and course syllabi.

Many counselors have never even heard of Glasser. It hasn't been until the last 20 years that his methods have become more and more respected and his concepts found to be solid and reputable. Today, we hear psychiatrists and professionals quoting him and making statements that Glasser had claimed 50 years ago as if they had invented them. He started out in chemical engineering and upon getting his degree, changed courses and became a Board Certified Psychiatrist with a medical degree.

The following are some of his latest acquired recognitions and awards. I had the pleasure of knowing and being certified in Reality Therapy and being in his company the last 12 years of his life.

Dr. William Glasser, M.D.
May 11 1925 - August 23, 2013

Professional Recognition of
William Glasser, M.D.

Since 1989, Dr. William Glasser has been recognized as a member of the distinguished faculty of pioneers in the psychological professions by the renowned Evolution of Psychotherapy Conference of the Milton Erickson Foundation.

In 1990, he was awarded the honorary degree Doctor of Humane Letters, Honoris Causa, from the University of San Francisco.

In 2002, he received the California Association of School Counselors award for his many years of contributions to the school counseling profession.

In 2003, he was presented with the American Counseling Association Professional Development Award in recognition of his significant contributions to the field of counseling.

The American Counseling Association presented him with a Legend in Counseling Award in 2004 for developing Realty Therapy.

In 2005, the American Psychotherapy Association presented him with the prestigious Master Therapist designation.

Also in 2005, he was presented with the Life Achievement Award by the International Center for the Study of Psychiatry and Psychology for his enormous influence as a psychotherapist and author.

In 2006, he was awarded the honorary degree of Doctorate of Education for Pacific Union College in Angwin, CA.

In 2008, the European Association of Psychotherapy publicly recognized Realty Therapy, which Dr. Glasser developed, as a scientifically validated psychotherapy and was officially announced at the twenty-ninth Annual William Glasser Institute International Conference held in Edinburgh, Scotland, in 2009.

In 2010, Case Western Reserve University conferred the Distinguished Alumni Award upon him.

Preface

This is my seventh book that deals with Dr. William Glasser's Choice Theory®, its concepts, and applications. Why do I write about Choice Theory when Dr. Glasser, himself, has written many more books than I have on something that he created? Why do I write about something that has already been written about several times?

When I first came across Dr. Glasser's book, "Choice Theory®," I couldn't put it down. I stayed up all night reading it. It was then that I felt I knew all about it. After all, I had just learned all about it by the Master, himself, by reading his book. I began to incorporate and apply what I had read in the book with my clients. I noticed it had very favorable results at first. Clients seemed to be more willing to talk about their situation and found hope for a better life by the time they left my office. But something was still escaping me. I didn't feel that I was able to help clients fully resolve their concerns. I had even completed a basic week of training with certified faculty of the William Glasser Institute but still had doubts about any success using CT as a counselor.

A year passed and I learned of a regional conference for Choice Theory to be held in Los Angeles. Even though I wasn't certified in Choice Theory, I attended. What I experienced was something I hadn't expected. Everyone there was so genuinely happy and real. There were people of every level of education yet no one cared to be impressed by titles or degrees. Everyone was looked upon as equal with no one being an expert. The room and all the people in it felt very "comfortable" and welcoming.

When asked what area that I applied Choice Theory, I informed them that my specialty was drug and alcohol abuse and addiction. I was immediately swarmed upon by many people there who wanted to know my procedure in using Choice Theory with that population. I told them that I wasn't even certified and had only completed a basic week of instruction yet that made no difference to them. They asked questions and began writing things down that I said while not learning anything that they didn't already know.

Another year passed and I discovered that Dr. Glasser and his wife, Carleen, were going to be lecturing on relationships and doing a workshop at a mental health conference in Las Vegas. I attended looking forward to meeting Dr. Glasser and having him autograph my copy of his book, "Choice Theory, A New Psychology for Personal Freedom." Having read his book, and having completed a basic week of training, and having attended a regional conference, I felt I had a fairly good grasp of Choice Theory before I was to hear him speak.

Once Dr. Glasser was introduced and began speaking, I soon discovered what I felt was missing in my understanding of Choice Theory. He explained it in layman's terms even though he was speaking to professionals. It all fell into place. All of the pieces of understanding that I possessed were not meshed together in all the right places when I read his book. It wasn't due to his writing skills. It had more to do with how I learned and processed information. I left the conference with my autographed copy of his book and my newfound excitement and understanding.

 What I had just learned and pieced together was so exhilarating that I immediately began sharing it with some of my colleagues who were continuing to practice the way we were all taught in school. They were reluctant to accept something that went against all they had been taught and doing with their clients. They had one question after another that tried to prove Choice Theory a naive form of treatment and a method to not be taken seriously. Their questions proved to do otherwise. It was almost as if they were a straight man for my presentation. I had an immediate answer to their questions that they didn't expect I could answer. They could see and hear the excitement in my voice over my newfound understanding of Choice Theory. But old habits are hard to break especially when they go against everything one studied and learned for four to six years or more.

I attended another Glasser West Region conference in Los Angeles and we were later invited to visit Dr. Glasser at his home in Los Angeles. Here was the man who was a world-renowned psychiatrist whom we students had to briefly study in college as the creator of Reality Therapy, and here I was sitting in his home talking with him!

I completed the advanced week of training and 6 months of practica in order to later become certified in Choice Theory. The next certification conference was held in Colorado Springs, CO. As was my usual modus operandi, I made an excuse for not going. I told my fellow Glasserians that I was in private practice and couldn't leave my office for four days and be away from my phones while in another state. Looking back, I always seemed to be able to come up with some reason as to why I didn't do something or other that would have been to my benefit.

I recall having learned in Choice Theory that if you wanted something but didn't have it, that one must do some self-evaluating and assess what they have been doing that was not working. It became apparent to me at that time that I had a history of alibis as to why I couldn't do this or couldn't do that. I changed my thinking to, "If you want something badly enough, you'll find a way to get it." I had a history of saying "no" to the things I should have been saying "yes" to. I found a way to put my practice on hold and made arrangements to attend the International Conference in Colorado Springs, participate in four days behavior of exercises to indicate my knowledge and ability to become certified. Dr. Glasser handed me my certification certificate on my birthday, July 16, 2008.

Dr. Glasser certifying the author in Reality Therapy

So after having read all of this story to this point, why do I continue to write on Choice Theory when it has been written about so often by both Dr. Glasser and other writers? We all tend to learn by way of different techniques. Some learn by listening. Others learn by seeing, while still others learn by hands on applications. Then there is the style of writing and differences in figures of speech that tend to be effective with some while not with others. I originally thought I knew all about Choice Theory by reading Dr. Glasser's book. I later discovered that it took Dr. Glasser's in-person lecture to make it all come together for me. So I had learned some of it by sight (reading) and then completed the knowledge by hearing him explain it.

It has been said, that we learn . . .

    10% of what we read

    20% of what we hear

    30% of what we see

    50% of what we both hear and see

    70% of what is discussed

    80% of what we experience personally

    95% of what we teach to someone else

I write about Choice Theory in a tone of conversation rather than being clinical. I also use my experience of relating real life examples from working with some of my clients to indicate and explain human behavior and Choice Theory applications. I am not so naive to believe that everyone who may read any of my books will find enlightenment but I do know that some readers will. This is why I continue to write about Choice Theory in a different style. With different examples . . . to reach the reader who follows and learns from my particular style over those of other writers who are just as qualified, if not more, than myself. I attempt to convey Dr. Glasser's ideas by writing and teaching them.

Since being certified, I have had the honor of presenting several lectures and workshops across the country on applications of Choice Theory with drug and alcohol clients and the importance of maintaining healthy relationships in helping others to find happiness. It is my sincere wish that what I have put into words will touch some of the readers of this book and empower them to enjoy a most fulfilling and rewarding life of happiness and serenity.

Chapter 1 - Why Did You Do That?

Throughout this book, you will become aware of how people think, perceive, and behave all for the sake of satisfying certain and specific happiness needs. You will be able to understand yourself more than ever before while, at the same time, coming to an understanding of how and why other people behave the way they do.

Some readers, as well as a few people in the psychiatric community, may think, "This is just common sense." Dr. Glasser's response to such remarks were, "My ideas are exceedingly un-common sense because they explain what to do when you don't know what to do." He explains that if his ideas were common sense, people would not choose to deal with their unhappiness by trying to control things that they can't control and continually choosing behaviors that are not effective.

You aren't "crazy." You're just unhappy. I have said many times that people do not seek counseling or therapy because they are so happy that they can't stand it. Every client I have ever seen came to me because something in their world was not the way they wanted it to be. Their unhappiness involved people, places, or things that were not satisfying to the degree that they wanted them. Their unhappiness could even be their own behaviors, which they had developed in their efforts to deal with their unhappiness. While many of my associates, doctors, and professional people in the psychiatric community may admit the reasons their clients came to them is because they are unhappy, they tend to not address their unhappiness with methods to resolve the source of their unhappiness.

What many in the medical and psychiatric community have been doing is looking at uncommon or unusual behaviors and attributing it to a medical condition as the cause of emotional problems and behaviors. They diagnose a person as having a "mental illness." Instead of discovering the source of a client's unhappiness, they opt for writing prescriptions that have no curative qualities but are effective in numbing the brain, sometimes permanently, with drugs that cause the person to simply not care about much of anything. Some even resort to electric shock treatments that induce seizures and destroy both happy and sad memories to deal with one's unhappiness. Prescription drugs change how the brain is to function normally. There is not a single drug that can have an effect on any one emotion without it affecting all emotions.

There are hundreds, nay thousands, of ways we can choose to get upset when things don't go the way we want them to go. Many frustrations, however, are superfluous and any unwanted and unhappy emotion that may result will tend to be short-lived and the situation quickly forgotten if not involving someone not important to them. Incidents of this nature are not the general cause of anything that results in long lasting unhappiness and aberrant behaviors.

The source of long-lasing unhappiness can usually be associated with those who are important individuals in one's world. It may be their parent(s), siblings, spouse or significant other, one's child, an employer, or even a teacher. When things aren't the way we want them to be, the natural tendency is to control it or take actions to "fix" the unhappy situation so that it satisfies how we want things to be. We function from day to day to satisfy our basic needs of happiness and pleasure. It's only natural to try to make any adverse situation more satisfying.

When nothing has been successful to make an unhappy situation happy, a person will often choose to become angry, or depress, and have intense feelings of frustration from repeated unsuccessful attempts to get their wants or needs satisfied. This is when they become creative and behave in ways they normally would not do. These newly created behaviors are intended to ease their unhappiness and frustration even if only to the slightest degree. These are the behaviors that others observe and declare to be "crazy" or the result of mental illness. To an unhappy person, even the slightest relief is better than no relief at all.

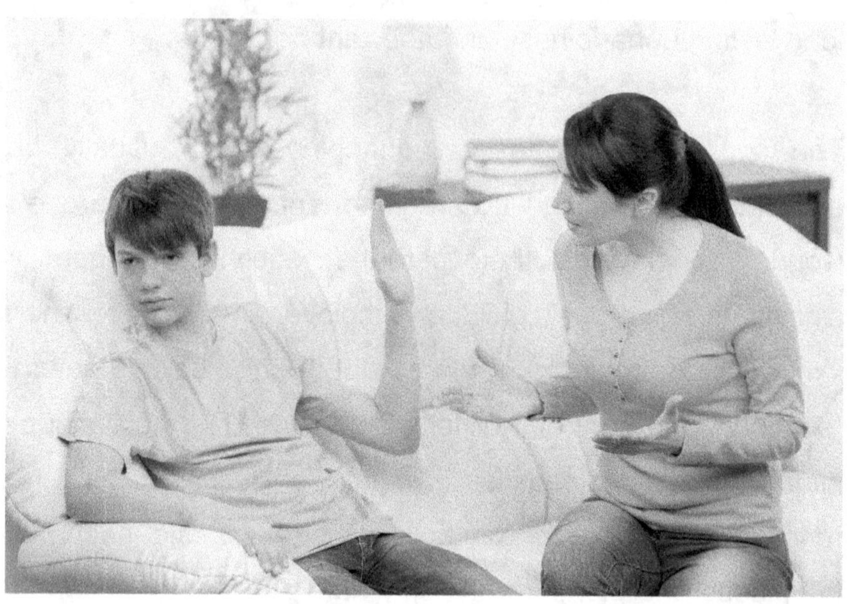

Have you ever wondered why some people do some of the things they do? Have you ever thought to yourself, "I wouldn't have done that" or even, "they must be mentally ill." Has anyone ever said to you, or have you even said to others, "If I were you, I would . . ." While it is true that none of us are the same, we humans do have far more in common with each other than you probably have ever considered, regardless of race, religion, gender, or culture.

What appears to confuse the issue of understanding others is that generally speaking, people don't understand what their own motivation is that may cause them to behave the way they do. If you don't t understand what motivates your own behavior, you will not be able to truly understand the behavior of others very well. We seem to be conditioned as "Human Doings" rather than "Human Beings." This may surprise some of you: We all have exactly the same needs, but to varying degrees, and different methods of acquiring them.

If you hope by reading this book that you will be able to learn how to change or control another person, you will be sadly disappointed and will fail to understand that the only person you can really control is yourself. Once you understand yourself, you will be able to see more clearly how and why other people do what they do. Knowing what makes you tick helps you to understand others, avoid conflict, and have a more consistent and happy life.

All plant and animal life is influenced by the information received from outside itself/ourselves. The difference being that in the plant world, they can't do anything about the external information they receive. They either adjust or perish. The more we go up the intelligence ladder, meaning animals with a brain, the more we can see how external information can be controlled to meet ones needs to some extent. If hungry or thirsty, food and water can be sought to satisfy those needs. If it's raining and we don't want to get wet, we can seek shelter, use an umbrella, and/or wear a raincoat.

In the animal/human world, the higher the intellect, the more behaviors can be created and utilized to meet external needs, but not without its share of limitations. For example, cats and dogs have only a few behaviors they can do and some are totally different from each other. They don't think of the future and they live only in the present. Dogs can't climb trees and meow and cats don't bark and sniff out drugs at airports. You get the idea. Each type of animal has their own limited, behaviors that they can perform . . . including us humans.

There is a limit to animal behaviors with human animals having the most. What separates us from other animals is that we have an opposable thumb, a more creative mind, can speak, write, plan, and invent things. While some animals have the ability to solve some obstacles they encounter, human minds have a wider range of skills to problem solve. We can also invent or create new problem solving measures. Humans also differ in that we have a higher understanding of "self" and our mortality.

Another thing that separates us from most of the other animals is that we always have a choice on how we react to any and all external information we receive. And this is the reason that differentiates humans from happy and successful people to unhappy and unsuccessful people and everything in between . . . the behaviors we choose, create, and utilize based upon our perception of the world outside us.

We all have the very same genetic needs for happiness. These needs are prevalent in all humans of all cultures and race. The deciding factor that makes us different is the importance and value placed on these needs. Where each of us is today on our happiness scale is the direct result of what we chose to do yesterday, now, and what we will choose to do tomorrow.

The needs I write about are genetic . . . meaning we are all hard-wired to have them as part of our being and our daily behavior. They are the reasons why we do the things we do from birth until death. As much as one may think they don't need these needs, the more they will not enjoy the life they desire to have. Some people have higher needs than others may have. But make no mistake; the need is still there regardless of the intensity and degree of the need.

While it is true that this applies to us all our lives, we are particularly self-centered right after birth. Newborn children care only for their own needs with little or no concern for others until they begin to reach the age of reason. It is at this time we recognize, and are taught by our parents and older siblings, that there are other people in our world besides ourselves and they, too, have needs of their own.

Even to the age of four, a child often has difficulty understanding the concept of others and their relationship to them in their life. Ask a child who has a brother, "Do you have a brother?' S/he will say, "uh huh." Then ask, "Does your brother have a brother?" S/he might very well reply, "No."

How well the lessons learned as children will depend upon the child's total environment, parental teaching, experiences, and their perception of them all. Some learn these lessons very slowly, or almost not at all, while others may learn gradually and continually for much of their lives.

Egocentric parents tend to develop egocentric children who care little to nothing for anyone but their own wants and needs. Loving, giving, sharing, sympathetic and empathetic parents tend to raise children with many of the same traits to various degrees. Our parental influence plays a major role in character and personality development. Our parents also taught us ways to deal with stress, anxiety, and unhappiness based upon how we observed the manner they dealt with them.

My intention is not to write a book about child development but merely to touch on the obvious to help you understand yourself and others better; learn new and more effective ways to resolve conflict, and find the path to maintaining happiness and a successful life.

Who you are, what you are, your happiness, your success, your good relationships, as well as your unhappiness, your failures, poor relationships, anger, anxiety, and stress are all the result of incoming Information that you observed or experienced outside yourself, how you perceive it, and how you choose to react to it. What happens outside ourselves may have an effect on our internal selves but only to the extent that we choose how we react to those outside events.

Whatever we may do to respond to the outside influence does not force us or cause us to react to it other than how we choose to do so. While you may not go through life answering phones that don't ring, you don't answer them until you do hear them. However . . . you answer the call only if you choose to answer the call. The phone didn't cause you to answer. You chose to do so. How many times have you refused to answer your phone when you didn't want to? It's a choice.

The choices we make are what contribute to our happiness or hell on earth. True, there are times when others may have performed transgressions towards you. Life is not always fair. What determines your happiness or sadness are the thoughts and actions you choose to manage those transgressions. You always have a choice in every situation.

While we are genetically predisposed to be guided by our genes for physical development, we have other genetic needs in order to survive and acquire happiness. We have little to no control over our bodily structured genes but over the many thousands of years, since humans first set foot on this planet, we have been struggling over a never-ending quest to control our genetic needs of survival, love and belonging, power, freedom, and fun. Thus, the creation of psychology . . .the study of human behavior. These are not needs that we constantly focus on every minute of every day. We seem to only become aware of them when we don't have them to the degree that we would like to have them.

While Abraham Maslow is known for his "Hierarchy of Needs" to attain what he calls "self-actualization," Dr. William Glasser has narrowed the human basic needs that motivate us and cause us to choose behaviors meant to satisfy the genetic needs for: Survival, Love and Belonging, Power, Freedom, and Fun. While some may find Wi-Fi to be a need, it isn't genetic.

Regardless of one's nationality, culture, social-economic, gender, or religious belief, these five needs are required by us all to possess whatever happiness is to us, individually, and why we say, think, and do all of the things that we do each minute of our lives.

General Dodonna was the first one to use the phrase, "May the Force be with you" in the 1977 release of Star Wars. He was speaking to the Rebel pilots before embarking on their battle mission. The inference being that the Force would protect them and encourage them to succeed in their efforts.

Since then, all subsequent Star Wars episodes have used this phrase and it has gone on to mean wishing someone good luck, good fortune, and for good things to happen.

It so happens that each of us have five innate forces within us that impel and motivate us to behave. These forces can be both positive and negative depending upon how we behave to maintain them. Dr. Glasser identifies them as the Five Basic Needs. They are in line with what could also be called today as, the five forces that drive our behavior. These forces are always with us and they are the motivation for everything that we do. The key to their success and happiness is dependent upon the behaviors we choose to satisfy them.

Some people enjoy outdoor activities while others would rather stay indoors. Some people like liver and onions while others may despise them. Some people like jazz while others may consider it noise and prefer classical, rap, or any other form of music. While some people find a certain genre of painting to be pleasing, others may not like it at all. Some may enjoy the aroma of coffee but not like the taste. Some may get pleasure out of petting a dog or cat while others may not care to be touched or are allergic to cats or dogs. Some choose to drink beer while others prefer to drink wine or distilled spirits, or choose not to drink at all. These are just some examples of how we are all different from one another. We are all the same species with the same needs but with different values, preferences, and strengths of these needs that motivate us to choose different behaviors.

The above examples are based upon the five senses from which we gather all our information: Sight, Sound, Smell, Taste, and Touch. Just look at the things that you like and dislike and assign which of the five senses that are attributed to them. Which of them gives you the feeling of happiness and/or pleasure and which of them do the opposite?

Who can say that because we care for or like certain things, values, people, places, etc., while others may see them differently, that they are wrong and we are right? The things that result in our personal happiness and pleasure are not all shared by everyone else.

"If everyone could learn that what is right for me does not make it right for anyone else, the world would be a much happier place." - William Glasser

Each of us possesses stored information of all of the things that lead to our happiness and unhappiness. We know what these things are. We have distinct images of what they look like. We place them in sort of a mental photo album, which

Dr. Glasser refers to as one's Quality World. We began to develop these images on the day we were born. The child who cries less often is the child who perceives his/her needs being met to their satisfaction.

On the opposite side of the non-crying child: There are some children whose needs rarely or never get met. They learn not to cry or rely on others to provide their needs.

There's the story of the child that from the day he was born, never cried and never even spoke a word even when he reached the age when most children begin to speak. His parents were very concerned and took him to several specialists who all informed them that they could find nothing wrong with their son's physical condition that would keep him from speaking. The older he became, the more his parents became concerned over his lack of speaking abilities.

One morning, when the boy was about seven years of age, he sat down to have his breakfast when he suddenly broke out with the words, "This toast is burnt all to hell!"

Astonished, his parents were both joyful and amazed. The father said, "Son . . . you haven't spoken a word from the day you were born until now. Why have you been so silent all of these years?"

The boy replied, "Up to now, everything's been okay."

When our perception of the outside world coincides with our internal world, "everything's okay." Our internal and external images match.

 We can even see images of those things that give us happiness or pleasure in our mind if asked to define them. If the information we receive from outside ourselves does not match the image we have inside ourselves in our Quality World images, we experience some form of glitch and know right away that something is not right for us.

Often, the tendency is to do something to control the situation to get the two images to match. It is at this point that we have conflict and disagreement with others or become even more frustrated because we are trying to control something of which we have no control.

I had been a professional musician for a good portion of my life. I happen to enjoy several different forms of music, but I am partial to jazz. Jazz is in my Quality World I have years of music education behind me and even more years playing and performing. In my Quality World, how can anyone not like jazz as much as I do?

The reason is simple. To those who lack the knowledge of musical structure, background, experience of playing, improvisation, and orchestrating, jazz may be unpleasant and misunderstood. I realize this so I don't get upset when someone tells me that they can't stand jazz. I feel the same as they do about other forms of music that they may prefer. I may find their musical choices to be too basic and simple with only a few chord changes. Our differences are in our perception, knowledge, and value placed upon the music. I don't dislike people because they don't like jazz music but if they do like it, I tend to like them more since we have something in common. But neither of us is right or wrong because of our different preferences to certain music genres.

People are drawn to one another by the similarity in their values (perceptions and beliefs). They remain together because of their similar interests. If jazz and some other form of music were the only differences a couple would have, it would hardly be worth breaking up because of it. But the more differences we have with one another, the more we increase the odds of conflict and a failed relationship.

> *"Don't marry someone you would not be friends with if there was no sex between you."- William Glasser*

All we do from birth until death is behave. And all behavior is chosen to satisfy happiness, pleasure, or both. We are constantly seeking happiness or pleasure each minute of our waking life. Our daily behavior is motivated toward satisfying these two emotional states of mind.

What's the difference between happiness and pleasure? One of the most common misconceptions that many people share is thinking that pleasure is the same as happiness . . . that they are one and the same. While pleasure may be a part of happiness, there is a marked difference between the two by way of how each is obtained and how long they last.

By far, the most intense emotion is pleasure. Pleasure has a major flaw. It is short-lived and the pleasure fades rather quickly. This is the primary reason why people tend to repeatedly do certain things that cause pleasure. Some of these repeated, pleasure-resulting behaviors are drugs, alcohol, sex, gambling, other repeated compulsive behaviors, video games, and out of control spending. The more unhappy a person chooses to feel, the more likely they are to resort to pleasure-seeking behaviors that serve to mask and distract their unhappy and frustrated thinking and subsequent unwanted emotions. In other words . . . to feel better.

Admittedly, some of the aforementioned behaviors eventually become more complex and often lead to biochemical dependency in the area of substance abuse. It's important to note that the above list of behavior choices do not require the involvement or equal participation of another person. They are behaviors that one may obtain by one's self without the aid of someone else. Pleasure can, and often is, acquired alone.

Happiness, on the other hand, requires the involvement of at least one other person, if not more. Unlike pleasure, happiness is long lasting and is sustained as long as you have one or more meaningful relationships. The more meaningful relationships a person has, the happier they will be. Take note of all of the things in the above paragraph that provides pleasure compared to what it takes to be happy. The simplest and best way to find happiness is via one thing . . . meaningful relationships with the important people in our lives.

Since meaningful relationships are the creation of happiness and good mental health, then the lack of relationships with those whom we want to have a meaningful relationship, or no relationships at all, will result in unhappiness. Others often create behaviors designed to control the situation and/or the other person to get them to behave the way in which we want them to behave with the intent of having a satisfying relationship. It's like forcing or controlling someone to like you. I have yet to see this behavior work successfully. It's easy to find someone to love. Finding someone to love us in return is the difficult part.

Chapter 2 - Why All Of Us Do Everything We Do

Over the years, we have created images in our mind of how we want things to be; those things that make us happy; our values; our likes of people, places, and things.

> *"All our behaviors are a constant attempt to reduce the difference between what we want (the pictures in our heads) and what we have (the way we see situations in the world)." - William Glasser*

Whenever we perceive an external image that is opposite of the image in our head that we want, one of three things tend to happen:

1. We try to take control of the situation, with as many ways as we can come up with, to *make* the images match so that we will be satisfied and happy.

2. We may simply accept the fact that the difference is what it is; beyond our control, and move on with our lives. Live and let live. We do this by changing what we are thinking about the situation and/or changing how we behave when we don't get the image we want.

While we do not have direct control over how we feel physically and emotionally, we do have direct control over our thoughts and behavior. These are choices that we have the ability to make. By doing either one, we have indirect control of how the situation makes us feel both physically and emotionally.

3. Refuse to accept the image that doesn't match our personal image and lash out in anger, or choose to depress and feel miserable, or come up with some behaviors that others can't imagine why we did what we did. While some people may do some strange or even illegal behaviors, they choose to do so because nothing else worked to ease their frustration and unhappiness at the time.

All behavior is chosen to serve a purpose of meeting a want or need. Those behaviors that are used the most are those that work to some degree for the user or they wouldn't do them. We may not see how some behaviors they choose works for them but they do.

Every behavior you and everyone else does, serves the purpose of satisfying a specific want or need at the time you do it. What is desired as a result of the behavior is to acquire happiness, pleasure, or both. That's it. I can't explain it any more simply than that. The only difference between you and anyone else seeking the same results is how each of you may choose different behaviors to satisfy whatever you want at the time.

Chapter 3 - How I Discovered Choice Theory

Just before I was to graduate from school, I had to complete several weeks of practicum. I was assigned to an agency that, at the time, was the largest behavioral health agency in the state. In the evening, I was to co-facilitate alcohol and drug clients in-group sessions. During the day, I was given an office to interview and assess clients from as young as 5 and as old as 80 for mental health problems.

I was very eager and excited to be doing what I was doing. For the first time in my life, I felt I was doing good for other people. The American Psychiatric Association (APA) publishes the Diagnostic and Statistical Manual of Mental Disorders (DSM). This is considered the psychiatric bible of identifying mental disorders of which the book has over 400 disorders. Ironically, the DSM admits that there are no known objective means to confirm abnormal brain activity for Schizophrenia, Bipolar, Attention Deficit or, Obsessive-Compulsive Disorder, or Personality Disorders. What this means is that diagnoses of these disorders, along with other psychiatric mental disorders, are determined by so-called experts based upon agreement of the criteria contained in the DSM. In other words, it is diagnosis by consensus and decree.

"Decades of psychiatric research have failed to establish a biological cause for any psychiatric condition. The lack of biological evidence is confirmed by the extraordinary fact that not a single psychiatric diagnosis can be confirmed by a biochemical, radiological, or other laboratory test." Terry Lynch, M.D.

At the time I was doing my practicum, I was not aware of this major fallacy of mental illness in the DSM. This was not taught or mentioned in any of my classes. So here I was, not even having finished schooling, and was assigned to diagnosing clients and referring them to our in-house counselors and/or psychiatrist based upon my findings of their behavior that matched the symptoms in the DSM. I can't begin to tell you how this was an ego booster. I was now a mental health "expert." I had memorized all of the major and most commonly considered mental illness symptoms listed in the DSM.

I was diagnosing eight to ten clients a day, each with only fifty minutes of time to complete and then write their case notes along with my findings in the remaining ten minutes of each session. Every client that I saw left my office with a DSM Axis I code assessment for mental illness and sent to the agency's counseling staff or to the psychiatrist to be placed on medication.

After only two weeks, I was approached by management and asked if I would be interested in being a full-time employed counselor. I think they may have asked because I had been increasing their client base, which increased their financial funding. So here was yet another ego booster: to think that a large mental health agency would hire me before I had even completed my practicum. I replied, "Sure, as long as I can also get credit for my practicum." Here I was with my first official employment as a behavioral health professional. I recall thinking to myself, "I must be pretty good at this profession for them to ask me to work for them before I had even formally finished my education." (One of my genetic needs for Power was being satisfied).

Several months passed and I began to think, "I know that the city of Mesa, AZ is a major city of over four hundred thousand people but I had no idea that so many of them were *mentally ill*. Could this be true?" It began to not feel right. Everyone cannot be mentally ill. I began to think that something else must be going on in people's lives that result in what we are calling "mental illness." The diagnoses were determined solely on subjective information with no objective testing of lab results to confirm an "illness" actually existed, and was conducted in less than one hour, and determined by the so-called "expert" . . . me.

I couldn't help but think that what I, and others in my profession, had been doing was diagnosing people with an illness they didn't have and have them prescribed medications for something that didn't exist.

It was this time that something totally serendipitous occurred. I was walking down the aisle in the psychology section of a major bookstore. Having been taught the nine major models of psychiatric approaches to therapy, I could tell by the titles of the books on the shelves of which modality of treatment the authors practiced and based their writing.

I came across a book that simply read on the spine, "Choice Theory - Glasser." I recalled having to learn the very basics of Glasser's "Reality Therapy" in school and I had not been impressed with it for two reasons:

1. Glasser didn't believe the past was important in a client's situation while most all other psychiatric modalities considered the past to be an integral part of a client's "mental illness." I had been taught that in school like everyone else in the psychiatric profession.

2. I didn't care for Reality Therapy because the teacher didn't know very much about it well enough to explain it and only skimmed over it.

This was a time when I doubted the authenticity of what was happening in mental health. I opened the book and began to read the first few pages. The first chapter was titled, "We Need A New Psychology." Glasser stated that "for all practical purposes, we choose everything we do, including the misery we feel."

I thought, "Well that certainly is different." I had more than enough misery and unhappiness in my life in the past to ever think that I was choosing to feel them. My curiosity led me to want to continue reading to see how and why he came to this conclusion. I couldn't put the book down once I started. I purchased it and read the entire book throughout the night. This was just what I was seeking to explain why any of us do the things we do and it is not because of any mental illness.

When anyone goes to school to become a psychiatrist, counselor, or therapist, they are not generally trained in any one modality of treatment. The core issues of counseling are taught along with some basic knowledge of different styles of psychology and then we all go out and counsel by the seat of our pants. The vast majority of those in the psychiatric community utilize an eclectic form of therapy by applications of several different modalities.

Today, colleges and universities have even forgone teaching counseling skills and are replacing it with pharmacology. Brain medicating is now considered to be the normal approach to helping clients with emotional problems. In a few short years, no therapist or psychiatrist will know how to do talk therapy and will, instead, prescribe mood altering, brain altering medications.

Having read Dr. Glasser's book, I came to the back matter of the book to notice that there was a web site for Dr. Glasser: http://www.wglasser.com. I went to the site and discovered that there was going to be a basic week of training the very next day in Phoenix. I immediately called and got the information and enrolled in the training.

After reading Dr. Glasser's book of Choice Theory and completing the Basic Week of training and six months of practicum, I believed I knew and understood all there was to know about Choice Theory. As it turned out, I only understood it on the surface and wasn't aware of it until I happen to attend conference in Las Vegas where Dr. Glasser would be lecturing. Listening to Dr. Glasser explain his concepts brought it all together for me.

I was so moved about what I had read and learned that I was bursting with excitement. I couldn't help but share what I had learned with some of my peers. This was the answer to the questions I had about how we have been treating what is being called *Mental Illness*.

My peers were not as enthusiastic as I was about Choice Theory when I told them about it and they doubted the efficacy of the theory. They, too, had been trained as I had been in believing that mental illness was a brain disorder and that everything that was causing people problems was all of the things they experienced in their past. Reality Therapy and Choice Theory is the antithesis of the theories that were being taught back then. Today, more and more professionals around the world are finding the work of Dr. Glasser to have been way ahead of his time.

After the Basic Week training, I moved up to the advanced week of training and another six months of practicum. Having completed the Advanced training, I was now eligible to become certified in Reality Therapy and Choice Theory. I had to attend a final week of training in Colorado Springs to insure that I qualified to be certified and Dr. Glasser presented me with my certification. Wow! While practically everyone in the psychiatric community relied on a cafeteria style or eclectic therapies . . . using the techniques of several different forms of psychology, I was certified in the form of psychology I use. Not only has Choice Theory had a major impact with my clients, it has also been a major part of my personal life that has resulted in happiness and peace of mind.

While the old die-hards of outdated psychiatric treatment is slowly fading, it is not so much the new dawn for Choice Theory. Those who are continually being taught the disease concept of mental illness are gaining in the use of prescribed medications for illnesses and mental/physical conditions that don't exist and making the pharmaceutical companies far wealthier than oil companies have ever been.

Psychiatry can cause more harm than good.

What has been done in the field of psychiatry for the last fifty years has been harmful in many ways. By taking the medical model approach to behavior, pharmacology companies began to create drugs that affected the brains of clients to control behavior. These drugs have no curative abilities but do cause the brain to function in ways that are not normal. They interfere with the brain's neurotransmitters and alter emotions and motor skills. Suddenly, doctors and psychiatrists began to rely on these drugs as a remedy and began prescribing them to their patients even when there were no laboratory tests to indicate a medical condition or abnormality existed.

Another contributing factor of harming clients is diagnosing them with an illness they don't have and labeling them with a mental disorder. This effect is twofold:

1. Clients begin to feel like they are no longer a "normal" person and are mentally flawed.

2. Other clients wear their labeled diagnosis almost like a medal of honor with a sense of pride. At least now, they feel they know what's wrong with them and they have an excuse for their past or not taking responsibility for any current behavior or improving their life.

Fifty years ago, any person who behaved differently and deemed to be mentally ill was looked upon as someone to avoid and possibly dangerous. No one wanted to talk about it. We even had mental institutions that housed those individuals who were having difficulty dealing with life. Once they were placed in what was called a "State Hospital," one could expect to be there for a very long time and go through hell to get released. Get them out of sight and circulation.

Lobotomies and electroconvulsive treatment (ECT) were common barbaric practices and ECT is still used today. Many lobotomies ended in death with no one ever being charged with murder. If they didn't die from the procedure, they were left practically vegetative. ECT sends electricity to the brain causing seizures and altering the brain's normal functioning as well as a lot of total loss of many past memories (good and bad). It is a procedure that should be considered illegal.

As long as mental health is governed and practiced under the medical model for treatment rather than as a public health issue, we cannot expect to see any advancement in improving mental health or those who need assistance.

Chapter 4 - The Basic Needs For Happiness

There are five areas of our life that are genetic in nature that contribute to all of our behavior regardless of culture. The more these areas are satisfied, the happier and more content we find our lives to be. Each of us has our own individual image of what it takes to satisfy these needs. The images people have in other countries may be markedly different from those of another culture but the same needs will be common regardless. Therefore, all behavior is designed to satisfy these images to the personal satisfaction of the one who wants them. These are the reasons you, and everyone else, do the things that you do on a day-to-day basis.

Glasser identified these basic needs as:

    Survival

    Love and Belonging

    Power

    Freedom

    Fun

You may have higher needs in some areas while someone else may have a lower need for the same area. As an example: A man who would like to have a wife and family, companionship, home, and be an active member of society will have stronger Love and Belonging needs than a person who is a confirmed bachelor and has little time for anything else. He may have even higher Freedom needs while the man who seeks marriage and family will have lower Freedom needs.

> *"All we do from birth until death is behave, and all behavior is chosen to satisfy happiness or pleasure."*
> *William Glasser*

Power

Of all the five needs, one of them appears to cause the most trouble when it comes to our ability to be able to get along with one another. Power is something we all need. It is not bad in and of itself. The problem it may cause is how it is used. Power can be both a creator and a destroyer of happiness.

Earlier I mentioned the role genes play in our development. They are the building blocks of certain traits such as hair and eye color, personality traits of fast, slow, or easy going; body shape and its changes over time and several other things. For the most part, nature takes care of these genes and turns them off and on at different times of our life. They are things that we have no control over and they happen when they happen. Other genes that affect aging and illness can become activated by things we ingest such as food and drugs as well as life-style.

Other elements of our power needs require that we satisfy our need to be appreciated, respected, compete, achieve, and succeed. We tend to produce and achieve more when we know we are appreciated and respected for our efforts. If you can find a way that causes others to respect you and your actions do not infringe upon the wants and needs of others, then you have found the greatest power you can achieve.

All animals tend to have a need for survival. Animals will fight to defend their territory, for food, and reproduction. Humans, however, will tend to fight over anything and everything. Other than survival needs, the genetic need for power over others appears to be unique only to humans.

So why do you, and I, and everyone else do any of the things we do? We want to satisfy these genetic needs that afford us happiness and or pleasure. Animals tend to know automatically what to do in order to survive. We humans, on the other hand, must learn how to survive. After we become independent from our primary care givers who taught us some of these skills, we must learn to deal with other dangers and situations that exist outside of our nuclear family bubble. We must also acquire an education and learn a skill or trade that allows us to earn an income so that we can afford shelter, food, clothing, transportation, and have our healthcare needs met.

While our genetic needs are hard-wired in each of us, the behaviors we choose to satisfy them are not built into us. We observe others, create methods, and learn how to satisfy these needs in both healthy and unhealthy ways.

We rise each morning, eat breakfast, shower, dress, and go to school or work, and interact with others. At noon we have lunch and then at the end of the workday, we drive or use some other form of transportation to go home, relax, and have dinner. We may mix with the family and friends at the end of the day and on our days off, we like to enjoy some form of recreation or fun.

And while we continue to survive from morning until night, there are other genetic needs we are attempting to satisfy from rising in the morning until evening slumber. Those other needs begin with the need mentioned earlier.

Survival - The Next Genetic Need

The will to survive is a very strong genetic need. Even one-celled amoebas will struggle to divide and survive. We humans have the survival needs of maintaining a healthy life, acquiring food, shelter, clothing, reproduction, transportation, and adequate finances to provide these and other needs. Survival needs can be diminished if, over time, continued forces such as isolation and severe emotional and/or physical trauma persist. Those who feel defeated or hopeless may consider taking their own life as a means to end their frustration and unhappiness. Most humans choose to withstand and/or find effective means to meet their survival needs without committing suicide.

Those with strong survival needs will do whatever they can to survive even under the most dire situations. Many a soldier wounded in battle with serious wounds may survive while a civilian, wounded in peacetime, may die of a lesser wound. The difference being that the solder has a profession where s/he knows being wounded is a distinct possibility and they may expect the possibility of it happening. Should they become wounded, it is no major surprise and they may have a tendency to fight to continue to live. The civilian, with a less serious wound, who may be wounded on the street does not expect to be wounded in a non-war situation. Should it happen, the shock alone may be so intense as to shut down some bodily functions and lead to a death that could have been avoided.

There tends to be the awareness of negative situations more than positive situations. I contend that this is part of our genetic need for survival. We tend to be more alert for danger or things that could bring possible physical and/or emotional harm. Some people seem to stay ready and alert in order to keep from having to get ready and alert. We are more on the alert for negative things than for positive things.

We are also aware of our mortality. We know that we will not live forever. Due to this awareness, there are those who are health-minded and take measures to be as healthy as they can. Medical science has also helped us to live longer lives than our previous ancestors. Then there are those who don't ever think of mortality and choose behaviors that hasten their demise over the long run for the sake of pleasure.

In the animal world, Mother Nature's genetic survival skills kick in at birth. Many of the newborn antelope family may be up and running within a matter of hours so as not to be victims of those who prey on them. Carnivores learn survival skills by observing their parent's and the built-in gene to stalk and hunt.

We humans have to learn how to get our five basic, genetic needs met. Nature doesn't hand them over to us as with other animals. Our survival skills are learned both by observing our parent's methods, their instruction and guidance, as well as acquiring an education that will provide finances for the continuation of getting survival needs met.

In the animal world, Power, another genetic need, is used to ward off other animals that might cause them harm; steal their food, defend their territory, or win the right to mate. This Power is utilized to insure their survival needs. Their Power is very basic and forceful and used to overpower other animals when their survival needs are threatened.

One of the most difficult addictions to deal with is the addiction to food. We need food to survive. Unlike the cessation of drug or alcohol used by addicts and alcoholics, people cannot cease eating or they will die. Food is often used to provide comfort. Most people die because of what they have been putting in their mouths and bodies. Heart disease, cancers, diabetes, liver cirrhosis and many other conditions are brought on by alcohol, drugs, sugars, artificial sugars, cigarette smoking, and the greatest threat of all . . . fatty foods.

I have a personal experience with over-eating and gaining weight when I stopped smoking. I became a "foodie." I took great joy in learning how to prepare exquisite meals that would be high priced items in a high-end restaurant. I particularly liked meals that had wine and butter sauces. Over time, I began to notice that I might be taller if I lay down.

When I finally saw the need and acquired the motivation to lose the weight, I couldn't help but notice all of the food ads on TV. I never paid much attention to these ads until I began dieting. Outside of a few dietary supplements advertised, almost all of the other food ads were of foods that would eventually lead to early graves if we did nothing but consume them on a regular basis. Hamburgers with cheese, bacon moist with grease, covered with a few healthy items such as tomatoes, lettuce, and mushrooms while being consumed by a scantily clad, voluptuous female would hit all the buttons of one's information receptors. You can almost taste, smell, and feel it as you see and hear about it on the screen. Ice creams, fried chicken, juicy steaks, fast foods, Vodkas, Rums, Wines, and Beer ads permeate the TV . Ironically, the other ads are for prescription and over-the-counter drugs to alleviate your symptoms directly and indirectly caused by all of the things you have been eating and drinking from all of the other ads.

Animals eat what they can to survive and not to deal with any emotional distress as many humans do. Nor do they diet or see a need to deprive themselves of food as do those who suffer from anorexia and obesity. In the wild, we don't see drug and alcohol addicted animals, overweight animals, anorexic animals, or animals that commit suicide. While there are those animals in the wild that die from lack of nutrition due to the loss or scarcity of their food source or illness, they don't willingly deprive themselves of food and drink. Animals that have no awareness of eventual mortality eat much healthier than we humans who know we will someday perish. We even go out of our way to consume foods and put things in our bodies that will accelerate our demise.

 While many animals have an automatic genetic impulse to hunt and acquire food, fly, swim, avoid danger, and reproduce, we humans must learn how to survive by learning what is safe and not safe to our physical wellbeing. We get an education to learn the basics of life and then go to college to learn how to specifically apply these special needs.

Education and experience leads to the acquisition of a skill or trade to be able to acquire employment that will allow for an income to provide food, shelter, transportation, and health. As for reproduction . . . that comes automatically by nature but artful and meaningful sex is something that must be learned.

Some students do well in school because it meets their Power needs for acceptance, recognition, and appreciation as well as self-satisfaction. Knowledge, as the saying goes, is power. A higher education teaches how to question our thinking and evaluate our thinking and others thoughts rather than merely accepting things as fact without evidence or proof. Those who drop out of school early and/or never receive a higher than a secondary education tend to be less knowledgeable and unable to process and apply information in a more beneficial way. This is not to infer that because one may lack a higher formal education that they will be inferior in any way. A person can learn everything about anything in five years or less with due diligence and on-going self-study and experience.

Other students may do poorly in school for any variety of reasons. They may be bored with the subjects being taught; have family issues going on in the home; the teacher(s) may not be skilled in dealing with the various needs of all students. Poverty and other environmental and emotional problems can also contribute to a student's ability to concentrate in a learning mode when stressed out or consumed in other more dominating concerns. These interruptions and distractions are why standard teaching methods don't work as a one-size-fits-all method in educating our youth.

Love & Belonging - the Third Basic Need

This is a very special need as I contend that when we satisfy our need for love and belonging, our efforts to acquire the other basic needs tend to come more easily. The power of love; poets and philosophers have been trying to describe love for thousands of years. There are many different forms of love that we strive to achieve. The Greeks have identified these different loves as follows:

1. Eros - Sexual, passion, and Desire. Named after the Greek god of fertility. In early Geek times, this type of love

was seen as dangerous and irrational, causing those who possessed it to lose control. Today, we see Eros love to be something to achieve. Instead of losing control, we may fall in love at first sight or fall head over heels in love with someone to be our lifelong mate. Of course, it can also be a negative force by seeking several mates with no intent other than to satisfy one's own needs.

2. Ludis - the playful love . . . what so many rely on before attaining Eros or sexual love. In the early stages of a relationship, we see it in the form of teasing or flirting. It is commonly seen during Happy Hour in bars laughing with friends, visiting others while playing trivia or other amusing behaviors. But mostly, it is the type of love that puts a little zing in our lives.

3. Philia - this type of love is a deep friendship or camaraderie with someone . . . Lifelong friends who have remained loyal to each other . . . those who have gone through good and bad times together, and those who have a special bromance . . . a kind of love and kindred spirit for one another that is not sexual in nature. It is also the love one may have for a specific group, society, or organization to satisfy the need to belong, fit in, and be accepted by others. There is also a sub division of Philia love called Storge, which is the love between parent and child.

4.   Agape Love - this is the love one feels for everyone. Many religions are based upon this type of love. While easily professed, it often seems to be forgotten or short-lived with cultures, societies, or individuals. The Golden Rule is based upon Agape love. Ideally it is a love for all mankind.

5. Pragma Love is a long-lasting love . . . a love between a couple that has endured for years due to their ability to compromise, be patient and tolerant to help insure the longevity of the relationship or marriage.

6. Philautia Love is the love of one's self. This can be either unhealthy and in the form of Narcissistic love or healthy in the form of widening one's openness and willingness to be secure, accept and like who they are which allows them a wider capacity for love for and from others. How you feel about yourself will determine how you feel about others. As the Beatles said, "And in the end, the love you take, is equal to the love you make."

We tend to go through life with varying degrees of these six forms of love. Some only acquire a couple of them and never seem to be able to acquire all of them at one time. As in life, love is always changing around us. We have a need to fit in, have friends, and hopefully have a long-lasting passionate and romantic marriage/relationship.

We want to belong to groups or organizations that have similar values and interests that we have. We seek out any number of denominational church, unions, clubs, organizations, groups, etc. We want to be around like-minded people or even learn what others think and believe.

We all have ways of getting our belonging needs met. We have our own group of friends with whom we associate regularly. Different religious denominations are groups of which many people choose to belong. There are labor unions as well as Alcoholics Anonymous, Cocaine Anonymous, Narcotics Anonymous, Co-dependents Anonymous, et al that are groups in which people feel they belong.

I belong to the William Glasser Institute of certified and like-minded certified counselors, therapists, psychologists, psychiatrists, educators, nurses, as well as those who are non-professionals who have become certified in Choice Theory.

Freedom - Our Fourth Genetic Need

Our freedom needs allow us to be able to make our own decisions and to do things on our own volition without being controlled or ordered by others; our ability to come and go as

we please and free from any confinements, both real or imagined.

In relationships, we must be willing to give up some of our freedoms as we now share our life with someone else. If we are absent and/or self-centered to have all things our way, the relationship will be short lived. We live in a society that allows for freedom while still having several laws, rules, regulations, and policies. If not for them, we might very well live a life of anarchy where everyone simply did whatever they pleased with no consequences for bad choices.

Yet we do have the freedom to choose to accept these laws, rules, etc and know that if they go against those of the democracy in which we live, we must be prepared to receive the consequences of going against them. I don't condone breaking the law, but we do have that free will to choose our behavior regardless of the consequences. Just ask any person in prison.

We want Love and Belonging yet we would have to give up some of our freedom in order to have them. Why? Because getting and receiving love and belonging requires the involvement of at least one other person. If we value our freedom needs more than our need to be connected, then those love and belonging needs would be very short lived.

Two people with high freedom needs will soon discover that their relationship or marriage will not last very long. If a person with high freedom needs has a partner with much lower freedom needs, there will be conflict as well. One will be more committed than the other in the relationship.

Freedom is one of the needs that tend to be taken for granted until some or all of one's freedoms have been taken away. Joni Mitchell reminds us in her song "You don't know what you've lost 'til it's gone." Those who have traveled to other countries where freedoms are restricted, always tend to feel liberated once they return home to the U.S..

I have a feral cat, that I have named, "Rocky." I call him that because he has a tip of his tail missing and there is a notch in his ear, probably the result of identifying that he has been neutered. When we first crossed paths, he was scrawny and dirty. He looked like he had been in a fight so I began to call him Rocky. He had been surviving by catching birds, which would explain the feathers I often found in my yard. He was

so scrawny and malnourished that his ribs were visible through his coat of fur. He has known nothing but a life of complete detachment from all humans and other cats. It's the only life he knows.

Rocky (after being fed a healthy diet.)

Living in Arizona, the summers here can be very brutal for animals that live outdoors and alone. They must survive as best they can. I began feeding Rocky every time he showed up at my patio door. He appears at 3:00 AM, which is when I am up and about, and again at 5:30 PM, which is when, I arrive home from my office. Somehow, his internal clock knows exactly what time of day those hours are. He even knows my different hours on Saturday and Sunday when I'm home all day.

It took several months before I could open my patio door to put food in his dish without him running away. In time, he learned that I had never attempted to harm him and he slowly began to sit nearby when I would drop food into his dish. Being a loner and with no other social group to belong (as cats are notorious for being independent and non-social), he appeared to suffer from anxiety and fear as evidenced by his paranoia. He could not find it in him to be able to relax and eat peacefully. He would eat a few bites and quickly look over his shoulder to see if anyone was coming up behind him or coming to steal his food. While he was free to roam and belonged only to nature; not confined, or locked up in a house, he was yet not free enough to enjoy his freedom without a price. He lives a life of nervous anxiety, distrust, and paranoia.

He has to endure extreme temperatures that he can barely stand. He would have to find a spot that had recently been irrigated and lay on the cool earth in some shade all day until the temperatures dropped. He could feel the cool air that would escape through my patio door when I opened it to feed him yet he would never set paw in my home that would provide him the comfort he would prefer to have. What causes Rocky to choose misery and strife in his life over being able to live in comfort in a temperature regulated environment that would also afford him protection, comfort, steady meals, love, and belonging?

The answer is twofold. Rocky has never known any life other than the one he has been living. He has developed several skills and has managed to get those skills to meet his survival needs. He is not aware that there are better and easier ways to survive and if he did . . . he would still not have a sense of connection or bonding with a human. He trusts no one and nothing. He lives in constant fear and anxiety of losing those things that he has been relying on for survival all this time. Secondly, this is his freedom and he is not willing to give it up even if it meant improving his life. As a counselor, I see similar types of behavior in humans and not just with Rocky. They have become so familiar with their situation that while they may not enjoy it, at least they know what to expect and are not willing to change for fear of the unknown. It's not a simple task to give up what one has been relying on for years in order to cope.

Rocky's idea of freedom is mostly instinctual and what he has created to be free and allow him to survive. Survival and freedom are Rocky's only concerns to the point that none of the other needs of love and belonging, power, and fun are important to him. In fact, those needs may very well be turned off. To achieve otherwise would be more stressful for him than he is willing to accept.

While we do live in a society of freedom, our freedoms are limited to the laws and culture in the environment and communities in which we live. There are some people in our society that don't have the freedoms that others have due to the fact that they come from other countries, race, gender, or religious differences. Our government criticizes and judges other countries for their lack of human rights yet we are no less guilty of inhuman rights. America is the land of the free if you are white, male, over the age of 18, and heterosexual. The point I wish to make here is that even our freedom is limited by certain criteria based upon what is acceptable and what is not.

> "Everything can be taken from a man but one thing: The last of the human freedoms—to choose one's attitude in any given set of circumstances, to choose one's own way." - Victor Frankl

Fun

One of the questions I always ask my clients when doing an evaluation or assessment is, "What do you do for fun and recreation?" I'm surprised after all these years when I still get a common reply of, "Not much. I don't have time for fun," or "I can't afford to have fun," or "I'm too tired to have fun." Those who tend to respond in this manner are typically addicts or alcoholics, people on disability, have legal, financial, or marital problems, and those who are depressing because someone in their life is not behaving the way they would like them to behave..

If their answer is any of the above reasons, I then ask, "What did you used to do for fun and recreation" or "If you were able to have fun and recreation, what would you do?" They usually come up with something. The reality is, even though some may say they don't have fun or recreate, they sometimes find a way to do so even if it is brief. We are genetically wired to have fun in our life else we would be forever miserable. Even highly depressing individuals have occasional good days where they have fun in some form or another.

There are so many ways to have fun that are dependent upon how we perceive certain activities as fun and the strength of one's need for fun.

Some people love to travel and learn about history and culture while others may find that form of fun to be uninteresting and even uncomfortable. Some people have talent for sporting activities while others may be physically incapacitated or not easily coordinated. Some people like to read while others may have never even read a book or know how to read. Some people require a lot of fun while others seem to get by with very little. I'm reminded of the parental saying, "Okay, you've had too much fun for today." How can anyone have too much fun? How much is too much? How does one measure fun?

Fun is how we learn. It begins with play. Even the play of young animals is a learning process for survival. Fun teaches us about fair play and getting along with others while obeying the rules and regulations of the fun activity. Without fun, we would not expand our knowledge and awareness. Our life would be mundane and bleak. Fun affords us relaxation from other demanding responsibilities.

Learning adds quality to our life. Looking back on your formal education, what was, your favorite subject in school? If I were to ask you why you enjoyed that subject so much, you might tell me it was because the teacher "made it fun," or "it was fun learning about the subject." When the teacher or the subject is fun, you tend to learn more about the subject than if it were boring, had a boring teacher, or was a subject in which you were disinterested.

While most of our genetic needs are handled by nature, our basic genetic needs for happiness are needs that we have to learn. They require action on our part and won't just happen automatically. We must find a way to have fun. Several of my friends love the game of watching professional baseball, which provides them with fun. I, on the other hand, find baseball to be boring. It moves too slowly for me to enjoy it. That doesn't mean they are wrong. It's their version of having fun while my idea of enjoyment and fun is doing something totally different. I prefer the fast action of watching football.

While there are many fans of NASCAR®, I continue to wonder what it is about that sport that draws so much interest. "Oh, look! He's making a left turn. Oh, Wow! He just made another left turn." The left turns at high speeds go on for hours. After two or three of them, I tend to lose interest. But that's me. There is something about that sport that others perceive and enjoy that I am obviously missing. Watching it and being present at the races satisfies one or more of their needs. Just because I don't care for it doesn't mean that I think that others should feel about it as I do.

Power Reprise

Of the five genetic needs, Power is often intertwined in some fashion or another in all of them. While I may write about the other four needs, you will notice how the use of power has both a positive or negative effect within all of them.

From the moment we are born, and perhaps even sooner, we begin to gather information from outside ourselves (our environment) by way of our senses of hearing, smelling, seeing, tasting, and feeling and immediately connect this information with how they affect us. We are unhappy, happy/content, or indifferent. For the first four years or so, much, if not all, of this external information serves to satisfy only our needs and no one else's. We are happy when we feel good and have what we want and unhappy when we feel badly and don't get what we want.

Infants learn about power very quickly. They discovered that to get the attention of someone to meet any of their needs, all they have to do is cry. The more unhappy infants are due to hunger, the need for a diaper change, or attention, the louder and more intense they cry that may result in quicker responses. They have learned that crying gives them power to get others to see to their needs. (Some adults continue this method). An experienced parent can often tell by the intensity or type of crying an infant makes what the child is wanting.

Power can be both productive and destructive.

Animals use power only for their survival needs. Humans will fight over the slightest little thing. There appears to be this need to be justifiably "right" about a belief, or value, or anything at all, to the point of fighting over it. There is also a strong urge to make the perceptions outside of themselves to match the image of what they want in their personal world if the two perceptions don't match.

When people's diplomatic skills are exhausted in their attempts to make their point; change another person's values or behavior, or get someone to do something they don't want to do, the use of verbal or physical force often comes into play. Those with the least amount of conflict resolution skills can feel so frustrated and offended that anyone else would dare see the world differently than they do, they may turn to physical force or even murder.

Every crime committed against humanity and every war that has ever been or currently ongoing is the result of power . . . using physical force or threats to get others to do what the aggressor wants them to do. Divorce is most often the result of using power unsuccessfully to get what one partner wanted. The commonly used power tools are criticizing, blaming, complaining, nagging, threatening, punishing, and even bribing or rewarding their partner to get them to do something that the other doesn't see the need to do or want to do. When one partner begins to use any of these methods, the other partner begins to use their own power tools in retaliation. These are the power tools that destroy what was once a loving relationship and destroy mutual love and respect.

Power can be both healthy and harmful. Everyone has the genetic need for power to some degree or another. Humans are a power- driven society. We want to have as much as we can get of those things that result in happiness or pleasure. We want success. We want to win. Professional sports have become the opiate of our country. We want our team to be # 1. Few sporting events exist that do not rely on power or control. We want to be the boss and manage other people. We want to get other people to do what we want them to do for our benefit. We want people to do things our way because we think we know better than they do.

People who have high power needs are sometimes over-achievers, or they can wield their power to the point of losing the things that mean the most to their success and happiness, i.e. their family and friends. The methods they use to get their Power needs met often result in pushing others away leaving others to have nothing but contempt for them. The person with only destructive ways to meet their high power needs may often put others down in order to bolster himself or herself. People with constructive ways to meet their high Power needs use their power to motivate themselves and accomplish things without infringing on the rights and needs of others.

It's important to note that not all high-powered individuals resort to maladaptive behaviors that take advantage or harm others. The drive to succeed requires a high need for power. However, the methods to succeed can be more easily accomplished with the help and support of others rather than the opposite. Power can be a motivator to accomplish, learn, teach, and create.

Society tends to admire the high achiever and highly successful individuals who have acquired financial success, material goods, and extravagant lifestyles most others can only hope to acquire. A common belief is that more is better . . . that if you don't have "more," you are either a failure or spinning your wheels getting nowhere.

Then there are those with medium to lower Power needs that are quite satisfied with what they have. They may strive for more but their level of Power needs doesn't drive them to compulsive or workaholic behaviors. Many financially successful people lead unhappy lives. Others, such as Microsoft's Bill Gates, Stock investor Warren Buffett, Entrepreneur Richard Branson, and TVs Oprah Winfrey are examples of wealthy individuals with high Power needs who use their power and success to help others as well as themselves. Then there are others with high Power needs that use their power to intimidate, threaten, punish, boast of their achievements (both real or imagined).

We are all motivated by the satisfaction levels of our basic needs. Whatever we perceive outside ourselves is merely information. From that information, we now have the opportunity to make a choice on how to react to this information. This external information is not what causes us to behave. We will always have choices on how we react to that information. . . in a manner that causes you distress, acceptance, or indifference. Your choice will determine your happiness or unhappiness.

Understanding these needs gives you a better knowledge of what motivates you and your behavior as well as understanding the behavior of everyone else. Once you understand these needs you can save yourself a lot of frustration when you stop trying to do things to get other people to do what you want them to do.

Positive Power

Although power can be used in detrimental ways, it can also have positive results. Power is positive when it affords us

some of the things we need for happiness. We can use our own inner power for motivation to achieve, accomplish, gain approval, succeed, compete, and create whereby the results will benefit, not only of ourselves, but also others. I get some of my power needs met by writing and selling my books. My Power needs also get met when I help others to discover their own happiness and learn ways to enhance their lives.

As a former musician/performer, I got my Power needs met by how well the audience received my performance both individually and for the other members of our group. When working for someone else, our power needs are met when our employers, managers, and coworkers recognize our efforts.

It is through Power that we deal with competition, success-fully dealing with others, inventing and discovering, and excelling in the creative arts. Power is acquired by choosing behaviors that result in others acceptance of us, our achievements, and attaining respect from others. When you receive the healthy respect from others, it doesn't matter that everyone may not respect you in this way. It only matters that you receive it from the important people in your life. We will never be all things to all people no matter how hard we may try. In fact, trying to please everyone is a sure way to find yourself on the analyst's couch.

When you truly respect other people, generally, people will return that respect back to you. I say "generally" because it doesn't always turn out this way. Others, who may be holding onto resentment from the past, or jealousy, may not be so willing to respect you. In their choice to remain angry or jealous, they are actually choosing to feel miserable on their own . . . not because you made them feel this way.

Their anger, resentment, and jealousy are emotions that they choose to have when they see or have a thought of you. This is when others may resort to negative power behaviors to attempt to satisfy their power needs. They deploy tactics to overpower or get the better of the person whom they resent. They may feel miserable due to their own thoughts and behaviors while you may be totally uninvolved or unconcerned. Their thoughts and behavior is like drinking poison and then waiting for the other person to die.

I am amused when I read the put-downs of others on social media. They want to insult people they don't even know in an effort to get them to see or believe the things they see or believe.

My Freedom needs are met by knowing Choice Theory and not getting caught up in other people's problems or allowing the negative opinion of others to affect my happiness and self-respect. I allow others the freedom to live the life they choose and expect the same from them. I can choose when I want to be alone and when I want to connect with others. I can make my own decisions and come and go as I please . . .although I admit I am somewhat of a workaholic and don't take time out for myself as much as I could. As long as my work habits don't infringe on the happiness and needs of others in my life, then my work schedule is not, by itself, a bad thing.

Not being in a current relationship allows me these more self-centered freedom behaviors. Should I become involved in a romantic relationship, I would have to give up some of these freedoms to some degree if I expect the relationship to last. If I choose not to, the relationship will encounter some rocky times and perhaps even end. Freedom becomes maladaptive when too much time with work or other interests interfere with time spent with family and friends.

My Fun needs are met because I love and enjoy my work with others and acquiring more knowledge of others and myself. Of course, I have other ways of getting my basic needs met besides my work. I get my Fun needs met doing the things I enjoy doing and not because I have to do them i.e. travel, gardening, attending Regional and National Conferences, preparing gourmet meals, music, writing, etc..

Basic Needs Assessment

In the graph below:

1. How important to you is each of the 5 Basic Needs from 1 to 5, with 1 being the least important and 5 being the most important? You can use the same number more than once for each Need. You don't have to use all the numbers from 1 to 5 - just the number of importance to you.

2. List from 1 to 5 (low to high) on each Need as to how you perceive that each need is currently being met in your life.

3. Place and " X "wherever there are more than 2 points difference from what you need and what you perceive you have. The greater the difference between the 2 numbers will indicate how serious the problem in that basic need is that needs attention.

	What I Need	What I Have
Survival		
Love & Belonging		
Power		
Freedom		
Fun		

Your Basic Needs are fairly constant. What you have and what is lacking will be changing many times throughout your life. But today, your responses are where you are today in your happiness schema. If you want to improve your life and find happiness, at least now you know precisely what areas of your life require your focus and attention. Keep in mind, any area will be something that you can change and improve yourself, and not dependent upon anything anyone else will do.

Your Relationship Needs Assessment

You can also utilize this diagram to see where your marriage or relationship stands with someone else in your life. Copy the diagram and have your significant other respond. Wherever there are 2 or more point differences between your Needs columns and your partner's needs will be areas of possible conflict in your relationship. The larger the point differences, the more serious the situation.

Possible areas of conflict

More than 2 points difference in your Survival needs indicates the person is not feeling financially secure or safe.

More than 2 points difference in one's Love and Belonging needs indicates the person is not receiving the love they want in the relationship. Again, the greater the difference between what one wants and what they feel they have, the more serious the situation.

A low power need vs. a high power need indicates one who may be complacent, unmotivated, or less aspiring while the other is just the opposite. An extremely high power and extremely low power indicates possible emotional/physical abuse.

Let's face it. Anytime we are involved in a relationship, both individuals will find it necessary to give up some of their freedom needs. There is another person in each other's lives so there will be a need for compromising and negotiating some of these needs for the consideration of the other person and the relationship. One who feels their freedom is compromised in the relationship will not be a happy person and tend to be more self-centered and self-gratifying.

Two people who both have high freedom needs will usually not have a lasting relationship as they both do not want to feel a loss of any of their freedoms to do what they want to do regardless of the other person. Two people with high Freedom needs are usually very reluctant to commit to a legally binding marriage. A High/Low freedom need rating often leads to one partner feeling the other may be cheating on them as they tend to do things on their own without the other person involved.

If one person has higher fun needs than the other, the one with the higher need will complain that the lower fun need person is a "stick in the mud" and " you never want to do anything I want to do. You're boring." Eventually the higher fun needed person will find ways of getting these fun needs met that could lead to distrust and conflict in the relationship. Wherever you find more than 2 points difference in your relationship assessment, it is highly important that whatever changes that need to be made are changes that you, alone, can do for the sake of the relationship and NOT what your partner can do for you. This is not an "I'll do this for you" and/or "you must do this for me" deal. It's a "what can I do for the sake of the relationship?"

Chapter 5 - The Destroyer Of Happiness

Trying to control others has been, and continues to be, the most destructive form of psychology that is used all over the world, in every culture imaginable. It has been relied upon since the beginning of mankind. After more than two hundred thousand years, you would think the world would wake up and say, "Hey! This stuff doesn't work too well and it causes more problems than it solves." But alas, only a small percentage of people have come to realize this. The behaviors used to control someone are the causes of every war, fight, disagreement, relationship/marriage breakups, murder, and all other crimes committed against humanity.

To recap: We all have these images in our brains of the things that make us happy and give purpose to our behavior. In other words, images of how we want things to be and how we think others should behave. If we perceive an image outside ourselves that does not match the image we have in our brain, it is human nature to try to control the situation by making the images match.

All information that comes from outside ourselves is received by our five senses, how we perceive it, and how we value it. If it is information that we wish to retain, we place it in our memory for future reference. If we find it boring or uninteresting, we treat it indifferently or may even disregard it totally.

Each of us is unique in what we find of interest or important. We cannot expect that everyone else will share our interests as much or even at all. While an NFL professional may not generally care for Tango dancing or another varied interest, there may be one or more who do like it. How you perceive information and use it to your benefit (or non-benefit) is based upon your interest and how important the information is to you.

> *"All of us perceive the world in terms of our own needs; none of us is capable of perceiving the world as it actually is. It will appear different to each of us because even though our basic needs are about the same, our specific needs from which all of us create our internal world are never the same."* - Wm Glasser.

> Glasser continues:
> *"We don't like people, even our husband or wife, if they dispute our view of the "world" because to us it is the real world and how dare they see it differently."*

He states that all we know of the real world is the information that we perceive via our sensory system.

> *"Everything else that we claim is the real world is in fact our own perceptions of that world, perceptions which we constantly try to change so that they coincide with the world in our head."*

All we give to other people, and all that other people and the world gives us, is information. We are constantly receiving external information from others, our environment, events occurring around us, and processing it, placing a value on it, and reacting to it in any number of ways based upon how closely it meets our perception of the world and our needs.

This book is a good example. It is nothing but information that you are acquiring simply because you are reading it (sight, and processing its value to you). While one reader may consider the information of great value, another reader may consider it to be boring, uninteresting, or disagree with it, and not glean much from it. In either case, how this information is received is the result a choice based upon the value one places on it and how the reader may perceive it as useful. It may be a way to improve their life, or having no benefit all based upon their perception. There are no physical or medical differences between the two different readers, nor are there any chemical imbalances in either of their brains that would affect them differently. Their differences are directed by their different perceptions and values as well as the knowledge they currently possess. And this is what makes us all so uniquely different from each other . . . our perception, knowledge, (or lack thereof), and values.

It is totally impossible to retain every bit of information that we receive every hour of every day. Otherwise, our heads might possibly explode. As Steven Wright has said, "You can't have everything. Where would you put it?" We retain what we want to remember based upon its importance to us. Since we receive a lot of information in our lives, we develop many behaviors to deal with it all.

What do we care about mostly with all the information that comes our way? Quite simply, the answer is determined by the reward of creating happiness or pleasure. People do what they do because it serves a purpose. If it didn't serve a purpose, there would be no need to do any behavior at all.

The information we receive either meets one or more of our basic genetic needs or it doesn't. Will this information bring happiness or pleasure or will it do the opposite? Again, it's a choice based upon perception and how we value it. If we like how we feel, we retain it as a positive reward. We store this information in our minds and refer to it often. We continue to choose the behaviors that result in the reward of feeling good and happy. If it causes unhappiness or displeasure, we retain it in our minds as something we chose not to want, or disagree with, which may lead to choosing behaviors that result in emotional and physical anguish.

Chapter 6 - Controlling Others

There are some things that we can, indeed, control but there are even more things that are beyond our control. When we become unhappy, the greatest cause seems to come from wanting, and failing, to control another person to get them to behave the way we want them to behave.

Have you ever had a relationship that didn't work out and ended badly? What was the reason it ended? One or both of you were trying to control the other person because they weren't behaving the way you wanted them to behave. You wanted them to do or be something they didn't want to do or be or they wanted you to do or be something other than what you wanted . . . Power.

At the beginning of your relationship, there isn't anything that either of you could do to cause you to breakup. You accepted each other as you were at the time and overlooked any disapproving behavior that either of you did. Sometime down the road, an attitude changed and one or both of you became unwilling to overlook any of the little shortcomings that you did when you were first fell in love.

In my work, I have found that a tremendous amount of individuals fail to recognize their propensity for controlling others. In fact, they would strongly deny doing any such thing. There are several ways in which people choose to control others and they have been doing it for so long that they fail to see their controlling behaviors as being harmful or even controlling. This is probably because they have been on the receiving end of being frequently controlled by others.

Methods to control someone else are behaviors that will result in the opposite of what one wants to happen either quickly or over a period of time. They distance you from the person on the receiving end and in no way will bring you closer together. The more one is subjected to these distancing behaviors, the more respect and/or love will die. No matter how madly in love you were in the beginning of your relationship, love and respect went out the window because of the following controlling and distancing behaviors:

- Criticizing
- Blaming
- Complaining
- Nagging
- Threatening
- Punishing

- Bribing and/or rewarding to control

Not only do these controlling behaviors harm romantic relationships, they also harm relationships with family members, co-workers, and everyone else who may be on the receiving end.

There are more than these seven behaviors that are used to control other people but these are often the most commonly used behaviors. Eliminating these behaviors will enhance one's life and relationships to a level they have only hoped for in the past and make life so much easier. These behaviors grow in overall usage when one person uses them on someone, the person on the receiving end will use them back on the criticizing person as their defense.

As Dr. Glasser reminds us,
"External Control begets External Control."

Criticizing

Over the years, each of us has developed many survival and problem resolution techniques that work for us, even if some of them are not completely effective. Some may be effective for the situation at hand but may cause other problems in other areas of life. After the accumulation of many of these perceived successful life-problem solving skills, one often develops an attitude of, "Not only do I know what's right for me . . . I know what's right for everyone." Once a person develops this attitude, they have automatically set themselves up for a lifetime of unhappiness and failed business, social, and romantic relationships involving several people in their life.

When you begin to give unsolicited advice; criticizing, or correcting others, or telling others what they "should" do, you are actually saying, "I know what's better for you than you do." How would you react if someone told you they know what's better for you than you? What may have had a positive result for you in your applications does not mean it will have a positive result for anyone else. Telling others what they need to do has the effect of distancing you from those with whom you want to help, especially if they haven't asked for your opinion. I'm reminded, once again, of Dr.Glasser's words of wisdom:

"If the world would realize that what is right for them is not right for everyone, the world would be a much happier place." - Wm Glasser

Most criticism is sincere and not meant to demean someone. Unfortunately, it rarely works as it points out shortcomings of the person who receives it. When pointing out something to another person, the wording can make all the difference in the world.   Careful wording can change criticism into a suggestion. The more a person is accurate in their criticism, the more damage it does. Criticizing the behavior more than the person, will have a better chance of effectiveness.

I can hear it now … someone reading this book is thinking, "But what about constructive criticism?" Criticism is criticism regardless of what name you call it. It is possible to suggest an alternative way of doing something without criticism. You can say something such as:

"Have you ever considered _________ " or

"What do you think might happen if you _________?"

Then say no more and leave it to the other person to decide or choose whatever they do next.

Criticism, regardless of its intent, depletes confidence and infers incompetency. Trying to please others adds pressure that typically results in failure. The more one is criticized, the more likely they are to give up and quit. Who criticized you the most over the years? How did you react to it? When was the last time you felt good after being criticized. How did you deal with it?

Those who were criticized the most tend to take even non -
critical suggestions as criticism, and become defensive
easily. Even simple teaching instructions, with no intent or
use of criticism, have been known to set off those who feel
they have been criticized and persecuted most of their life.
Consequently, they may have a very low sense of self-worth,
which they cover up by applying their own forceful controlling
behaviors.

Alan, the son of one of my associates, is in his mid-forties,
divorced, on disability, who feels he has been wronged by
practically everyone in his life . . . mostly by his mother,
father, and his stepfather. He suffers from anxiety and often
strikes out at others on social media whenever he feels
stressed, victimized, or on the receiving end of the external
controlling behaviors. He lashes out with long missives that
could normally be stated in a few sentences. He has low
self-esteem, which he tries to mask by commenting on
things of which he really doesn't know. Mostly, he lashes out
against his mother. He wants her to feel as miserable as he
does because of what he perceives, real or imagined, she
and her husband have done to him. When riled, he will even
lash out at others he barely knows and even strangers on
social media. When he hurts, he wants others to feel pain
as well. He tries to hide his pain by causing others to

concentrate on the pain he inflicts on them verbally. . . Power.

Want he really wants is to feel a sense of love and belonging yet he chooses behaviors that push people away, especially those most likely to connect with him. He is in conflict with his genetic need for love and belonging by choosing behaviors that he perceives as easing his frustration while, at the same time, those behavior distance him from those who would provide his needs. He could just as well be saying, "I love you, I need you, get away from me!"

When he verbally strikes out at his mother, he finds himself fighting his genetic bond with her and he feels his shame and guilt over what he says and does to her. This only adds to his unhappiness and low self-worth, shame, and guilt. He goes back and forth between blaming her (and others) and then blaming himself.

Because he sees himself as "something wrong," he experiences anxiety attacks when in the company of others since he fears they will discover his perception of being a faulty person. Criticism from others came often to him in his youth. Because he believes the important people in his life look at him disapprovingly, then everyone else does so as well.

The slightest benign suggestion is perceived by him to be an attack on his intelligence and character. He refuses to take any instructional direction of any kind, which is one reason why he dropped out of school. His perception of being taught is that of being told what to do . . . something he may have experienced often from the important people in his life during development. Authority does not fare will with him.

Until he decides to stop playing the victim role and begins to take responsibility for his own life and happiness, his life won't change. He will continue to live a very unhappy existence . . . living a nightmare of his own creation. He sees his unhappiness as the fault of everyone else except his own.

He suffers from social anxiety believing people are looking at him disapprovingly. He wants desperately to be successful at something . . . anything . . . but realizes that he doesn't have the education to get him to where he wants to be. This is another reason he uses to lash out at those who are educated and resist their help. He doesn't have what they have, reminding him of his perceived shortcomings. Being in public and socializing with strangers or casual acquaintances tends to increase his anxiety. He fears being "discovered" as being inept.

The most harming criticism comes from our own self-talk. Our own criticism keeps us from becoming and achieving the very things we want to have, do, and be. We can be our own worst enemy. Our self-criticism reminds us that we may be inept, a failure, and incapable of achieving the things that would make us happy. We say things to ourselves that we wouldn't say to our own enemies.

It appears that self-criticism might serve us to recognize our shortcomings so that we can improve. What it does, though, often reinforces our negative self-image and keeps us stuck with little to no improvement. While we can get away from others who criticize us, we cannot run away from ourselves.

Years ago, when I was a traveling musician, many people would come up to me after the performance and compliment me on my playing ability. I didn't take compliments very well back then because of the image I held of myself. To me, someone who could play on the levels of a Clark Terry, Chet Baker, et al were those who earned the compliments and I, in my mind, was nowhere near their skills. I would always thank the person who complimented me but my self talk was, "Thanks, but what the hell do you know? I don't play anywhere near the way I'd like to play."

One night, after a performance, a well-know musician, who also plays the same type instrument I played, said to me, "Hey, Man. You play a nice horn." I said, "Thank you," and the voice in my head began to repeat the same message I have played over and over, "but what the hell do you . . .?" I stopped in mid thought. He DOES know! So maybe I do play a nice horn after all. I recall I went back on stage for the next set and played better than I had in my entire life.

Our self-talk is meant to ease the tension and stress of our errors or lack of skills. Ironically, it can only add more. We may take self-criticism as a direct affront to character and not on our behavior. This is why it is so damaging to our self-image.

The heaviest use of criticism on a child is at school for not "living up to your potential," for bad grades that are considered below expectations and standards of both parent and teacher. Yet another area that criticism exists by not living up to a parent's or coach's standards of athletic ability in soccer games, baseball, and other team sports and little league games.

A young lady of my acquaintance lost her father a year ago. She posted on Facebook: "Twelve more days before I have the most miserable day of the year." She was referring to the anniversary date of her father's death and declaring how she will behave on that day. She is actually setting herself up to have a miserable and sad day by counting the days before she chooses to have her "most miserable day of the year".

The closer she got to the date, the more she began to experience physical health problems. What she was anticipating and perceiving not only was choosing to feel severely depressed, but also having an indirect effect on her physical health. Rather than celebrate her father's life and their time together as a family, she chose to think and feel the opposite. Why would she do this?

She was experiencing a loss and that loss is self-centered. She focused on what she no longer had which is understandable yet a rather selfish thought.

Her announcement that the sad day was coming was also a way of informing others to come to her pity party and commiserate with her while hoping to get love and sympathy at the same time. This does not mean she is mentally ill. But it does mean she is preparing and choosing to be mentally unhappy, needing and wanting empathy and sympathy from others, and feeling sorry for herself.

Grief is a natural emotion that we will all experience and is unavoidable unless you are a sociopath who does not value anyone's life including your own. There is also no time limit as to when a person's grief should end but the more we grieve our loss, the more we stay stuck in sadness and an unsatisfying life of our own. Acceptance is the time we come face to face with reality of our own mortality and that of others. When we lose someone close to us, our grief is the price we pay for love.

Dr. Seuss wrote: "Don't cry because it's over. Smile because it happened." Recalling the good times and all of your happy memories of one who was close to you will have you feeling much better than living in misery and self-pity.

Self-talk creates self-prophecy. She has just as much power to choose not to feel badly in twelve days as she does to choose otherwise.

Here is a Buddhist Vision: "If you focus on the hurt, you will continue to suffer. If you focus on the lesson, you will continue to grow."

Blaming

Blaming runs a close second to Criticizing and being deadly. It puts the cause of one's unhappiness on the other person, while at the same time, piling on shame and guilt. To one who already has a low value of him/herself, this can be very hurtful and add more harm to an existing fragile ego. Blaming another person with no factual evidence can get really old.

For example, a wife who continually accuses her husband of being unfaithful when he hasn't may eventually lead the husband to decide he's had enough. Her continuing to accuse him of something he hasn't done causes him to lose respect for her as well as any love he felt for her so he eventually may think, "I've been accused of cheating for so long, I may as well do it."

If the wife ever does discover his unfaithfulness, she will say, "See? I told you, you were cheating on me!" In such a case, her continual jealousy and blaming actually made it easy to choose to do what she has been accusing him of doing. She didn't make him cheat. He chose to do so because he has been accused of it so often and he wasn't getting his love needs met with his wife.

As a behavioral health counselor, I have encountered more seemingly complex and different client situations than you can imagine. All of my clients come to me because of one thing: They are unhappy. I have yet to have a client make an appointment to see me because they were happier than they could tolerate. In every scenario, the root cause of their unhappiness is always an unsatisfying relationship with someone important to them. The unhappy relationship may also be an unhappy relationship with one's self.

Unhappiness is also something that is ongoing, right now, in the present, even though it may have started some time ago. When someone has tried all that they know how to do to find happiness in a relationship and nothing they do seems to help, this is when my phone rings.

More times than not, the client wants to blame the other person for his or her own unhappiness. Their perception of the problem is that the other person is not behaving the way they want them to behave; or the other person is trying to get them (the client) to do something they don't want to do; or they are both trying to get each other to do what neither of them want to do. It is an age-old tactic of trying to control someone to get them to behave in a manner in which they want them to behave.

They perceive their problem as being caused by someone else and not anything they, themselves, are doing. "If only s/he would change" or "If only I could get him/her to do what I want, I would be happy." Wanting or waiting for someone else to change or to do what you want them to do when they don't want to do it; or if they don't see the need to change or want to do what you want them to do, will keep you waiting for a long time with no changes made at all.

I also have clients who have gotten into trouble with the law and are required to comply with any number of requirements to satisfy the courts and/or agency in which they must comply. When they choose not to do what they are ordered to do, they continue to blame "the system" or others for their troubles.

An example of this would be the client who lost his driver's license for a year or more due to having an illegal substance in his/her system when driving. To have their license reinstated, they must complete an evaluation by a qualified Chemical Dependency therapist who will determine upon completion of the evaluation, if that person appears safe for their license to be reinstated.

My evaluations generally consist of at least three standardized questionnaires as well as a minimum of 20 minutes of one-on-one interview. If the questionnaire scores and interview are acceptable and corroborate, then the client has their license reinstated. However, if the client makes several errors due to not listening to the oral instructions as well as the written instructions for completing the questionnaires; has conflicting responses between the written questions and oral responses; continues to use or abuse; or lies in their responses, then the evaluation will end in an unfavorable ruling on their reinstatement.

Many times, those who are denied will blame the legal system, the MVD, and most often, me, the evaluator, for causing them all of their trouble in not getting their license reinstated. It doesn't matter to them that it was their choice to use drugs or drink beyond the legal limit that caused them to lose their license. They blame all of their troubles on other people and situations while not taking into consideration that it is their own past as well as current behavior that led to their loss of license and failure to get reinstated.

I have been threatened physically, accused of male sexual molestation, received phone harassment, had my windows shattered with bricks, given bad reviews on search engines and social media, and threatened with law suits because they failed to indicate they were no longer abusing or addicted. I have even been accused of making things up and altering their written responses and twisting their words that would keep them from being reinstated.

Choice Theory explanation: They didn't get what they wanted. In their Quality World, they had an image of driving again and that they would get their driver's license reinstated because they perceived themselves safe for reinstatement, or because they believed they could fool me into believing they were safe for reinstatement. They didn't get the image they had in their Quality World when they were denied reinstatement so they resorted to trying to control me and deploy any power procedure they could devise.

In all fairness, many of the clients that I deny understand why they were denied and take responsibility even though they may be less than happy about my denying them. Many try to fool me, thinking they are smarter than I. They don't take into consideration the years of study and experience I have with evaluating those with substance abuse behaviors and seeing what they believe they are hiding from me. About thirty-per cent of the clients I deny are not willing to take responsibility for their reason for denial. I am perceived as the person who is the roadblock to their happiness and the cause of their anger and disappointment. They feel helpless and victimized by "the system" and "some guy who doesn't know what the hell he's talking about."

My denial of their reinstatement did not match their image of themselves being able to drive legally with a license that would contribute to their happiness. There are some who believe they can do something about their unhappiness by, somehow, trying to make my life miserable or cause problems for me. It is their creativity, which will be covered later on, that leads to the behavior choices they make that they may inflict upon me. What are the chances that their choices to "get even" will cause me to change my evaluation to get their license reinstated?

Their emotional state of choosing anger is overriding their thinking and behavior. Rather than helping them with their cause to get their license reinstated, it is doing the opposite and contributing more to their unhappiness. They resort to power to try to control their unhappiness without realizing the power methods they choose are making their situation worse.

They have lost some of their Survival needs to have adequate transportation and perhaps to even be able to have a better paying job since they cannot drive to their employment. Their financial needs are also affected without their license.

They have lost their Freedom needs by not having the capability to drive to places and do things they may wish to do. They are not having much Fun with limited ability for connecting with others for fun and recreation. It's understandable that their anger may be directed towards me. I'm perceived as the villain who is keeping them from their happiness.

Their choices of behaving and thinking are the cause of their unhappiness and not due to external causes or because of someone else. I don't make them feel or behave the way they choose. It is their own behavior that makes them unsafe for reinstatement yet they won't accept that and find it easier to blame me. They don't consider that I may be saving them from killing innocent people, or even their selves, by continued use of drugs or alcohol while driving.

Many clients I have seen will adamantly declare that other individuals are the cause of their unhappiness. Children, both young and old, will blame their parents, a sibling, or a teacher. Parent(s) may blame a child for their unhappiness. A husband/wife will blame their spouse as the cause of their unhappiness.

Blaming someone else for your own unhappiness will keep you stuck in the role of a victim. Feeling like a victim of someone else's behavior will never allow you to move forward and take charge of your own life. It will only give power and control of your life to the person you feel is victimizing you.

I often get calls from many a wife who is complaining about her husband's drinking. Who has the problem? Most of you may say, "The husband. . . because of his drinking." If he didn't drink, she would be happy (external perception). Actually, the wife is the one with the problem.

Marie called me because of her boyfriend, Paul's drinking. Who has the problem? It was Marie who called so she is the one with the problem. Paul didn't call me. If I were to ask Paul if he had a problem, he would be sure to tell me that Marie is the one with the problem, not him. And he would be correct.

While Paul surely may have an alcohol problem, he doesn't perceive his drinking as a problem. So the person who is having the most difficulty dealing with it is Marie. When I ask her what she has been doing to deal with his drinking, she told me that she has criticized him and called him names attacking his character; blaming him for all of her unhappiness; complaining and nagging incessantly; threatening to leave him if he didn't stop (mostly a threat); and punishing him by not talking to him (Addicts and alcoholics loves things that don't talk back so Paul would welcome this option), and not sleeping with him. She may even bribe him in some manner to get him to stop drinking. When I asked her how effective any of these methods were, she emphatically told me that not only did they not work, but that he would drink even more when she did these things.

It isn't what is happening externally to you. It's how you perceive and choose to react to what is happening internally to you. Any and all of your unhappiness, anger, sorrow, anxiety, etc is coming from inside of yourself and not from outside of yourself. You always have a choice in how you want to react and feel about a situation. There is a space between thinking and doing. In that split second space lays the opportunity for you to choose how to react.

In the above scenario of Paul's alcoholism, Marie has been trying to control his behavior with externally controlled methods. Not only do these methods fail to get the wanted results, they keep her in the role of a victim . . . blaming him for her unhappiness. He is addicted to alcohol and she is addicted to him. She has this seemingly uncontrollable urge to take measures to get him to stop drinking. Not only do her methods fail, they increase her frustration and anger worse had she done nothing.

If someone in your life is behaving in a way in which you disapprove, the first person who needs to change is you.

"When we are no longer able to change a situation, we are challenged to change ourselves." - Victor Frankl

If the things you have been saying and doing to control the other person to behave the way you want them to behave, and none of your methods have been effective in getting the results you want, why keep doing what doesn't work?

Complaining

Have you ever been around someone who seems to do nothing but complain? They tend to find fault with others and many things, even things that may not be very important. Their world is perceived of existing with a lot of negativity and it has somewhat blinded their ability to see the good of someone or something. They may not complain about you but if you associate with them for any period of time, they will eventually complain about you too. Nagging and complaining go rather hand in hand.

Jonathan came to me because he was unhappy in his marriage. From what you have read so far, you will notice that the problem, before I even tell you his story, is that someone is trying to control him, or he is trying to control his wife, or they are each trying to control each other.

Jonathan is an artist. He has always been an artist all of his life starting in his childhood. He loved art or any kind. He went to college to study art and worked for other people as an artist and graphic designer when he graduated. He felt he was never allowed to express his own artistic talents while working for others.

When he got married, his wife knew he was an artist and that was his vocation. While she didn't necessarily share his interest, he did bring home a weekly paycheck. Jonathan wasn't making a lot of money but he was able to support his wife and their two children.

Jonathan eventually tired of not being able to utilize his talents while working for someone else. He had put aside enough to live on for several months and decided to go out on his own. His motivation was power, survival, and freedom. The effect it had on his wife was that his decision to go out on his own threatened her security and survival needs. He struggled and for every progressive step he took, it seemed like something would happen to set him back two or more steps. The money became tight. He was still making a few dollars here and there and his wife had to get a job to help out financially. Her stress and anxiety began to increase because her marriage image was not matching the image she had in her mind of a happy marriage. She began to utilize the controlling behaviors in an attempt to make the marriage images match.

Jonathan reports that his wife began complaining about the decision he made to go out into the art world on his own. He also disclosed that his mother-in-law would also complain to his wife that she didn't approve of his career choice. He stated that from the moment he would wake each morning until he went to bed each night that she would complain and criticize him. He stated, "She would often say things like, "Why aren't you a lawyer? Why aren't you a pro golfer? Why aren't you a doctor?" He stated that every day she would have another occupation to complain that he hadn't chosen in life. "What she was basically saying was telling me that she didn't like my career and criticized me for not having what she perceived to be a more lucrative and more admirable profession. My career was not acceptable to her or her mother."

I asked him how he dealt with that each day. He said, "She would leave for work and I would just ignore her comments. She knew I was an artist when she met me. She married me knowing I was an artist. So why did she marry me if she wasn't satisfied with my occupation?"

I asked, "Did you ever make that point with her?"

He replied, "Yes. After several months of tolerating it, I finally told her that she had always known what I did for a living so why begin complaining about it now? Each time she would say things like that to me, it was like saying, and "I don't approve of what you do for a living." Her mother also would criticize me to her daughter which urged my wife to criticize and complain even more so. It was a total lack of support from the one whom I needed it the most. Each day she chipped away at my self-respect until I had hardly anything left. The more she criticized, nagged, and complained, the more I could not concentrate and focus and the worse things got financially. I soon began to lose my interest in her and what I was doing and just gave up. I lost my motivation and hope for success. Why bust my butt to succeed if what I do is not appreciated from those I need it the most?"

I asked Jonathan what he wanted to achieve by seeing me and he said, "I want you to tell me what to do." I informed

Jonathan that he would need to make his own decisions based upon our discovering the different choices he has and ways to deal with his wife's behavior. I asked if he wanted to stay married and he said, "I don't know if I want to after all of the hurt. She doesn't respect me anymore and I have obviously lost all my respect for her." I asked him, "is there any love left for her at all?" He said, "Truthfully? No."

Even if Jonathan chose to stay in his marriage the way he felt, he would be unhappy the way things are. I asked, "Does your wife want to stay married? Has she stated that she has considered a divorce?" He stated, "Yes, she has but I don't know if she was serious or not." I explained that I can show couples how to stay married only if they want to be married and aren't just seeking counseling as a last resort, especially if they have already decided to divorce.

Since Jonathan said he no longer loves and respects his wife and since people don't usually talk about divorce unless they are serious about leaving as did his wife, I didn't hold much faith in them benefiting from counseling. They had both pretty much made up their minds that the marriage was over. Neither respected the other and when respect is gone in a relationship, love is gone as well. There's no need to give them false hope and take their money and spend my time trying to salvage a marriage where love and respect no longer existed between them.

I said to Jonathan, "I believe you already know what you want to do. You just want to hear it from me to justify your decision. It's not easy to end a marriage, especially if there are children, but you also have to consider what is best for everyone involved. You and your wife deserve to be happy yet it appears that this is not going to happen. You can continue to live with your marriage the way it is with both being unhappy; you can change careers but while that may make your wife happy, you would continue to be miserable and possibly hold a lot of resentment toward her. If you both sincerely want the marriage to work, and I do mean sincerely, then I will be more than happy to help you both out and show you how to mend it."

I didn't expect to hear back from Jonathan, and of course, I didn't. The long term criticizing and complaining he was getting had destroyed whatever love and respect they once had for each other.

Nagging

"If I've told you once, I've told you a hundred times . . . " This may come as a total shock to you but they heard you the first time. Telling someone ninety-nine more times will not get someone to do something they don't want to do. Actually, the more you nag someone to do something, the more they are likely to not do what you want them to do even if they know they would be better off in doing it. Simply stated, it's annoying. And anything annoying is not what anyone wants to do.

Constant criticizing, as in the case of Jonathan and his wife, is also nagging. He was constantly being reminded that his career was not acceptable to her and complained by asking him why he wasn't "this" or "that."

Maria constantly nagged Paul about his drinking in order to get him to stop. She admitted that it only made him drink more.

Threatening

Threatening is a behavior with the intent of manipulating the other person to do something they don't want  to do. And if they refuse, "there will be consequences." Threats come in many different forms and they are all based upon power. " If you don't ______________ , I'll leave you." Or, "I'll tell others about you." Or, "I'll divorce you and take the kids." Or, "I'll close all our financial accounts." Or, "I'll hit you." And the deadliest of all, "I'll kill you." Again . . . these are all words of power to control someone. The common response to threats is, "Just try and see what happens," a counter-threat. Power begetting more Power.

I have been threatened with possible lawsuits several times by clients whose driver's license I denied from being reinstated. The standard threat: "I've talked to my lawyer and you can expect to hear from him very soon." I have never heard from any lawyer in over twenty-three years.

Punishing

There are several ways in which punishment is delivered dependent upon who is on the receiving end. A parent may resort to "Time Out" with a child, spanking, beating, and even torturing. One parent I know of had her child wear a pig snout mask and sit on the curb of a busy street with a sign that read, "I disobeyed my mother." The method the mother chose was to embarrass and publicly humiliate her child while believing her method of punishment would "teach him a lesson." It would, indeed. It would teach the child not to trust her mother, lose any respect for her, as well as destroying the child's self-worth and image that could leave a lifetime of scars. This is one of those examples of where one choice of action to control another person may satisfy the parent, but will cause the child to have a very unhappy life. The old saw, "It's for your own good" can destroy a child's self-worth.

When punishing another adult, some common methods are physical force, cutting off sexual relations, and the old standby . . . not talking . . . the silent treatment. Not talking is communication. It conveys the message, "I'm angry with you and don't want to talk to you."

We live in a punishment based society. Society says if you break a law you need to be punished. The idea is that punishment is used for the purpose of deterring people from breaking rules and laws and also to stop any offenders from reoffending.

It's against the law to kill someone and if you do, we'll kill you. Punishment has done little to deter crime. The DUI laws in Arizona are designed to hurt your billfold, embarrass you by spending a minimum of 10 days in jail, and get an interlock device in your car for your first offence. This form of punishment was designed to deter one from getting another DUI. While it may be effective for a few, it has been my experience that many young drinkers think it's a joke and continue to drink and drive and get additional DUI arrests with even greater consequences.

Ironically, punishment has also been a common behavior to get others to produce more. In the old movies, we would see Egyptians beating exhausted workers to get them to move the large blocks of stones to create the pyramids. Then there were the slaves who rowed the large ships across the seas who were whipped for being weak and not rowing hard or fast enough. So if someone is ill, weak, or incapable of performing a certain task, what sense does it make to beat them to make them even more incapacitated and perhaps even die? Not only did the punishment fail, it caused more problems because they are now a man short of completing the task.

Animals, as well as humans, often become more angry and defiant and lash out when they have been continually punished. Our prison system is filled mostly with re-offenders and if released, often continue their crimes against humanity as a result of their punishing treatment and anger.

Bribing/Rewarding To Control

Bribing, of course, is a method to get someone to do something they don't want to do that will result in some form of reward if they do what is desired by the briber. Rewards are often in the form of cash. In sales, the rewards to bribe workers to increase output are cash, jewelry, trips/vacations, cars, high tech items, and paid time off. "If you do this for me, I will do this for you." Quid quo pro with a prize. Bribing is essentially using someone to satisfy any one or more of one's genetic needs. It does little to provide respect and does more towards resentment.

Rewarding, however, can be positive. Tipping someone for going above and beyond what may be expected or for something not particularly asked for is a win/win situation. I recall Bill Harrah of Harrah's of Nevada casinos having a philosophy of paying people more than they expected. His philosophy was that in doing so, it would help keep employees loyal to the job, they would be more willing to be productive and reluctant to leave the job. This would save him time and money to retrain new personnel. It would also instill in a worker to produce more when they are recognized as someone who is worth more and not because they were ordered or bribed to produce more. I think rewards are great if not used to coerce or manipulate a person to do something they would rather not do or don't know how to do.

Our purpose in life is to serve others, regardless of what we do for a living. If those who serve us do more than generally expected, I have no problem in rewarding them with a tip above the normal tipping scale. Successful billionaire businessman, Richard Branson states: "Clients do not come first. Employees come first. If you take care of your employees, they will take care of the clients."

When Bribing and Rewarding are used to control others, then it is a distancing behavior that often results in conflict.

When you stop using the seven distancing behaviors, your relationships with everyone will be the best you have ever experienced. Not only will others in your life treat you differently but you will find yourself being a better and much happier person. Don't just stop doing them on those close to you. Stop doing them with those who even might be giving you a hard time. Replace them with the seven caring habits.

The Ultimate Question

If I say or do _______________________ *(you fill in the blank)*

Will it bring us closer together *(Caring Habits)* or

Will it push us further apart *(Deadly Habits)*

Seven Deadly Habits	Seven Caring Habits
Criticizing	Supporting
Blaming	Encouraging
Complaining	Listening
Nagging	Accepting
Threatening	Trusting
Punishing	Respecting
Rewarding to control	Negotiating

Chapter 7 - Our Tool Box & Creativity

Another recap before proceeding: We receive information from outside ourselves, determine its value to us, and compare it to the images in our mind of the things that make us happy. If it matches our brain's image in our Quality World, then we are happy and it meets one or more of our basic and genetic needs that impel us to behave. If the image does not match and fails to satisfy one or more of our basic and genetic needs, we try to "make" it match the image that we want. We try to control it. If the situation involves another person, the usual procedure is to use the distancing behaviors to control them to get what we want from them (usually with disastrous results).

If the perceived information fails to meet our needs, we feel any number of emotions as well as physical effects such as stress, tension, upset stomach, perspiration, nervousness, aches, pains, and tears dependent upon how important the situation is to us at the time.

This is when we reach into our bag of tricks, or tools, that we have learned and gathered over the years to deal with unhappy situations. Some of these tools were taught to us. Some we found by accident while yet others were learned by observing how other people may have dealt with their unhappiness.

The most common maladaptive tools we may choose when the distancing behaviors fail, and when all else fails, is to turn to drugs, alcohol, violence, and suicide. The first two numb unwanted emotions and thoughts, and the third will numb and/or overpower the person who is perceived as being the cause of the frustration. It may even result in death of one or the other. And the last choice will end it all quickly. The more effective tools we have for addressing conflict and happiness, the happier we will be in our life. Limited tools lead to limited choices.

Life is full of disappointing situations. It isn't so much of what happens to us as to how we deal with what happens in our life. The rain falls on all of us at several times in our life.

So what does a person do when all of their tools have not worked and their frustration has grown more intense as a result of their unresolved situation? They get creative. They make new tools. This brings us to our next topic of understanding ourselves and others called:

When we have tried all of our tools that we use to make our unhappy perception of the external world meet the image we have in our brain to make us happy, we rely on our creativity to make new tools hoping that any one of them will be effective.

An example would be after you have had a disagreement with someone whose point of view does not meet your point of view. You both may have argued to the point of the discussion escalating to name calling, talking over each other, refusing to hear each other's point of view, etc and end up walking away unsatisfied with your results. We've all experienced at one time or another. Several minutes, or even hours later, you say to yourself, "I should have said _____ or _____." That is your creative mind at work after all your other tools failed to satisfy your want and need to win your argument. (Power).

Here's another example that I'm fairly sure you can relate to. Have you ever done something that in hindsight you thought to yourself, "Boy, that was really stupid"? It may be stupid to you now but at the time, it seemed to be the best choice you had when you did it. I have a friend who told me that she once placed the legs of a ladder on two paint cans so that she could level the ladder on her staircase to reach an area to paint. It was her creativity that solved the problem she faced on how to reach the area she wanted to paint. Looking back on it, she admits it was not the smartest move and could have ended disastrously. But it was the best idea she had <u>at the time</u> to solve her problem . . . to complete her project of painting the stairwell.

Our creativity is what is behind all of the behaviors that others may see as mental illness. When one is frustrated to the point that they have used all of the skills they know that have not been successful in meeting their needs and duplicating the image in their mind of how they want and think things should be, they begin to create new behaviors. These behaviors may not be any more successful than those that failed but they will, to some degree, ease their frustration somehow and in some way.

The Five Basic Needs and Creativity In Action

So much of the world appears to be caught up in the belief that any behavior that is not considered usual or normal is the result of a mental illness . . . that there is some sort of "chemical imbalance" in some people's brains. I am often challenged in my group sessions about the behavior of those who have been labeled schizophrenics, when I state that most of what we are calling mental illness is no more than the behavior of unhappy people who are struggling to get their happiness needs met. Even those who have received this diagnosis have challenged me on this statement. They seem to want to let others know they are helpless and that there is nothing they can do to improve their happiness. I often hear, "Normal people don't talk to themselves; see things that aren't there. So there HAS to be *something wrong with their brain.*"

Those who have received mental illness diagnoses have been told that they have some abnormality within their brain and that there is nothing they can do about it . . . that they will have to learn to live with it for the rest of their lives while taking medications that drug their brains to cause them to not hear voices and stop seeing invisible people, etc..

These drugs also stop the person from functioning normally by shutting down all of their emotions; having a flat affect; losing interest in the things that they used to enjoy,'; creating irreparable physical conditions, and losing their ability to be creative. Ironically, many of these medications prevent the person from overcoming their unhappiness by shutting down the mind's creative ability to deal with and resolve their unhappiness.

Some behaviors are considered to be mental illness by some circumstances, but not mental illness in other circumstances. Allow me to explain:

I enjoy movies. As a behavioral health practitioner, I notice all of the different dramatic situations and how the actors portray their talents and methods in dealing with their particular situations. Art imitates life and life imitates art.

One of my favorite movies that I use to explain how we use creativity and choose our behavior is the movie "Cast Away" featuring Tom Hanks.

After being marooned on a small island in the South Pacific, following a plane crash, Chuck (Tom Hanks) was unable to get his basic genetic needs for happiness met. He had to be creative to survive and began to improvise ways to provide shelter, food, and to hydrate. He soon found himself without the power to do much about his situation but maintained enough power from within to continue to survive. Even when he considered suicide, his tested method failed and renewed his internal power for survival

 Chuck's freedom (a basic genetic need for happiness) was now very limited. He had only a small portion of the island in which he could navigate as most of it was rugged, mountainous, and surrounded by pounding waves. He was held in solitary confinement. He certainly was not having any fun (another genetic need for happiness). All of his basic needs for happiness were not being met to the degree that he wanted.

The first thing he did when he reached the island after his plane crash was to yell out to connect to someone . . . anyone. Even the sound of dropping coconuts led him to think that someone might be near and he would yell out towards the area where he heard the sounds. He was missing the genetic need for connecting with others and belonging to the social world he had recently lost. He still had the image of Love in his Quality World from his deeply satisfying relationship with his girlfriend, Kelly (Helen Hunt), back in Memphis.

From what I have described so far, and for you who have seen the movie, you would not think any of Chuck's behaviors were the result of a mental illness. In fact, you would probably think that it was his creativity and improvisation that was able to allow him the ability to meet his needs of survival: shelter, food, and drink.

But it wasn't long after his initial awareness that he was, indeed, stranded in the middle of nowhere and the odds of being rescued were minimal. He still had the strong genetic need for love and belonging (a genetic need for happiness) and after injuring his hand while attempting to make fire, his frustration led to him choosing to throw objects that had washed up from the plane crash, kick the sand, swear, and destroy whatever was near him. His bloody hand from the injury he incurred left a palm print on a volleyball that had been part of the cargo in the plane.

He eventually created fire and was so elated that he proclaimed to the sky and the sea of his accomplishment in boisterous pronouncements. "Look what I have created! I have made fire!" His power needs were beginning to be met giving him a better sense of accomplishment and success.

After he had calmed down and successfully created the fire, he began staring at the volleyball and saw the potential for something in the bloody hand print . . . a human face. Since no one was around to offer a need satisfying relationship in the form of connecting with others, he would create his own person to meet this need.

He made the air hole the nose and erased some of the blood to make the eyes and mouth. The company who made the volleyball was Wilson and the company name was boldly printed on the ball. This became Chuck's compensation for connecting with someone whom he named, "Wilson." So far, you may be saying to yourself, "So . . .? What's your point?"

Chuck then began talking to Wilson and even answering on Wilson's behalf to satisfy his need for love and belonging and connecting. And I would be willing to wager that you would still be thinking, "Well, sure. There's nothing wrong with that. He did it to keep his sanity . . . to keep him from going crazy on a deserted island . . . to connect with something or someone when no one else was there to connect with" **AHA!**

If Chuck behaved like that back in Memphis where he lived, would you still say his behavior was an acceptable way to behave? One might be inclined to get as far away from him as possible because, "who knows what a crazy person who talks to himself or to inanimate objects might do?" One might also believe he is seriously mentally ill and should be placed on brain meds and in dire need of a psychiatrist.

In an isolating experience, you are more likely to accept Chuck's unusual or unnatural behavior as typical, rational, and understandable. But if not deserted on a lonely island, the same behaviors are seen as symptoms of mental illness and chemical imbalances. The unusual behavior one may create and perform serves the purpose of easing their unhappiness and frustration, at the time . . . just like Chuck on the island. If he didn't have Wilson to talk to, and imagine that Wilson was talking to him, he would have felt much more unhappy and frustrated than if he hadn't created Wilson.

 The person who sees things, hears things, and talks to people who are not present, or to inanimate objects, is no different than Chuck. While they are not physically on a deserted island, they are in a deserted world based upon their choice to isolate or detach from others because of unsatisfying relationships with the important people in their life. They have detached from others and can be alone while around others. Their creativity to deal with their frustration and unhappiness is no different than Chuck's creativity in producing and talking to Wilson, a volleyball.

Often, one's frustration is the result of wanting to do one thing with their life while others who are important to them want them to do something else. They may attempt to take both routes and find it impossible to do. Consequently, they may become so frustrated that they then choose to take neither route and isolate even more, which further destroys their need for love and belonging. And since love and belonging are basic genetic needs, they create their own people in their mind and imagination like Chuck did.

The only difference is the circumstances. You could see Chuck's dilemma and rationalize Chuck's behavior because you could relate to being in his situation. Since you could relate, you deem it normal, acceptable, and not a mental illness at all. You were living in his world on the screen and silently thinking, "I'd probably do the same thing."

If Chuck behaved in this manner back in Memphis, you would not see the situation he would be experiencing in his world. His unsatisfying situation and internal frustration would be very real to him but invisible to you. Since you have most of your needs met, on a somewhat regular basis, in a world where they are more easily attainable than a desert island, you might be inclined to think and believe Chuck's behavior is a mental illness.

When Chuck was rescued and came back home, he didn't talk to things or people who weren't there anymore. First of all, Wilson was lost at sea before he was rescued. When Chuck got home, he was back in a world with people with whom he could connect . . . and it didn't take brain meds to get him to stop talking to imaginary things or hearing imaginary voices. He only had to connect with others and those who are important to him. After five years of living in isolation, his rescue not only saved his life, it restored most of his basic genetic needs for happiness: Survival, Love and

Belonging, Freedom, Power, and Fun. The love of his life had given up hope for his return and had married someone else. There would obviously be some emotional pain from that loss because he had maintained the picture of her in his Quality World all those years. But even losing Kelly didn't cause Chuck to return to his island surviving behaviors.

 Would you say a child who has an imaginary playmate is mentally ill? Or would you say they are being really creative? I had an imaginary playmate as a child. But I was so moody that he wouldn't have anything to do with me.

When you dream at night . . . are some of your dreams really "out there?" Does that mean that you are crazy when you are dreaming or is your mind simply being creative? If your brain can create these things when you are asleep, it is also capable of doing it when you are awake.

In our world, it appears it is much easier to convince others that a person is mentally ill than to convince them that they are sane and only frustrated and unhappy due to unsatisfying relationships with the important people in their life.

There is no chemical imbalance or external situations that cause us to behave. We choose our behavior to deal with these external events. The lack of nicotine didn't make me eat ice cream when I quit smoking. I chose to do so because I like ice cream and it gave me pleasure. Smoking altered my mood. Calm as long as I smoked, and edgy when I didn't. The edginess was the result of the lack of nicotine withdrawal. Ice cream replaced my need for a nicotine mood stabilizer. People don't depress, have anxiety attacks, strike out in anger, obsess or have compulsive behaviors, etc because of external situations. They do so because, in some way, unseen by others, these choices ease their unhappiness and frustration from how they are experiencing and perceiving these external situations.

Since behaviors are chosen, we Glasserians refer to the chosen behavior as verbs or gerunds. Something is going on in a person's life that they are stressing, anxieting, depressing, angering, obsessing, etc. to deal with their unhappiness. What is it that can cause a person to choose such behaviors? Outside of natural disasters or living in war-torn or impoverished environment, the reason why people have created behaviors that appear odd or out of the ordinary is: Relationship Problems.

They are not experiencing the relationship they would like to have with someone who is important to them. They have tried all that they know and if all has failed, they create ways in which to deal with their unhappiness and frustration. Who are these people with whom they lack the relationship they would like to have? They are: Their parent(s), their spouse or significant other, siblings, teachers, perhaps an employer, coworkers, student peers, or perhaps even their selves. That's pretty much it. . . unsatisfying relationships with the important people in one's life.

The behaviors that one develops may not completely result in the happiness or the pleasure they desire but they may result in lessening the frustration and unhappiness they are experiencing by not having the satisfactory relationship they seek. Some examples of these developed behaviors are anxiety, depression, obsessive/compulsive behaviors, paranoia, somatoform illness, schizophrenia, uncontrolled anger, and substance abuse. Rather than having meaningful relationships for happiness and good mental health, unsatisfying relationships are the result of unhappiness and poor mental health.

"The most common way people express their unhappiness is through aches and pains." William Glasser

Unhappiness affects the immune system and makes one susceptible to infections and other ailments ranging from headaches, Fibromyalgia, to more serious conditions such as rashes, cancer, pneumonia, gastrological problems, hypertension, sleep problems, excessive weight gain or loss, etc, etc.

"All long term emotional problems are relationship problems." - William Glasser.

There are those, including many of my friends and associates, who believe that some behaviors are so "far out" that they *have* to be the cause of a brain disorder or mental illness. The most common "mental illness" they refer to in their discussions with me is schizophrenia. I often hear people say, "No one acts like that unless they are mentally ill." "You can't cure schizophrenia with talk therapy. They have to be put on psychiatric medication."

There is not one psychiatric drug that has ever "cured" anyone of any so-called mental illness. No psych meds can isolate any single unwanted emotion without having some form of an effect on all emotions. Very few prescription drugs can cure any medical condition that is not caused by an infection.

One's creativity is how they overcome their times of adversity as well as their times of success. Pharmaceutical drugs, alcohol, and street drugs impair the ability to be creative and keep one in a state of unhappiness. You won't find many people who have ever been "cured" of their mental illness by taking psych meds or attaining and maintaining success while addicted to drugs or alcohol.

It is one's creativity that leads them to create certain behaviors that effectively diminish their frustration that others declare to be mental illness. As crazy as their behavior may be to others, it gives a sense of control to the person who uses them. While their behavior does not resolve their unhappiness, it does provide a modicum of relief.

Chapter 8 - Total Behavior

All we do from birth until death is behave . . . and all behavior serves to satisfy happiness and/or pleasure. As I write these words, I am behaving in several different ways at once. I am breathing. My brain is thinking and creating. My heart is pumping blood and oxygen from the air my lungs take in to keep my brain functioning and controlling all of my other bodily functions of emotions, thinking, and behaving . My digestive system is functioning. My eyes are viewing and processing my monitor for sentence structure and written concepts. My hands are typing words. I'm hearing things around me. And I'm thinking about what it is that I want to convey by putting my thoughts into words to share with my readers. It gives me pleasure to write. I enjoy it and it also serves to reinforce my beliefs and values of life, happiness, and peace of mind. I feel happy knowing that I hear nice things from my readers who tell me that my words and those of Dr. Glasser have had an impact on their lives. Just look at all the behavior that is going on all at once in my world right now. Talk about multi-tasking. Our body and brain are behaving even when we are sleeping.

One of the most damaging concepts and destroyer of happiness that many people believe is that other people, and things outside of themselves, "make" them do the things they do (behave). Here are just a few of the things that people say that supports this belief:

> "Don't make me mad."
> "Don't make me hit you."
> "Don't make me do something I don't want to do."
> "You really piss me off."
> "You make me happy."
> "You made me do it."
> "I wouldn't have done that if you hadn't <u>(fill in the blank).</u>
> "You gave me no choice."

We always have a choice …always. All behavior is chosen and purposeful except for those physical and uncontrollable behaviors that may be caused by neurological problems such as Tourette's Syndrome, Parkinson's Disease, mental retardation, Alzheimer's, cerebral palsy, etc.

The outside world only provides us with information based upon how we perceive what we see, hear, taste, smell, and touch. Information does not make us behave. It only gives us information that we then process and choose to react in any number of different ways.

When we hear or think of the word, "behavior," the tendency is to identify it with observing someone's actions and identifying it as some form of verb or gerund. While this is true, there is more to behavior than meets the eye. Behavior is the result of thinking, feeling, doing, and experiencing some form of active biology within both the mind and body.

If I am hungry, my body tells me so physically. My brain informs me that I have several options to satisfy my hunger. I can choose to partake of something I may have available at home; I can go out to a fast food or nice restaurant; I can prepare something in the kitchen, or I can call for delivery. I have no direct control of my hunger without first thinking about how I can satisfy it.

Without my thoughts of how to satisfy my hunger, I would remain hungry and possibly even starve. Once I have chosen what I want to eat and how to acquire it, I then take direct control by acting to satisfy the need. I may feel anxious in a nice way, or any other emotion in anticipation of what I am about to receive and enjoy that will satisfy my hunger. I can see the image of what I want to consume in my Quality World. This emotion doesn't just happen. It occurs because of what I am thinking and the images I have of those things that I like to eat.

Any emotion we experience is the direct result of what we are thinking at the time. You can't have an emotion, negative or positive, without first having a thought. For those who suffer from anxiety, depression, anger, stress, or fear, what are you thinking? Your emotions are the direct result of your thoughts at the time. Both your thoughts and emotions will have some affect on your body either internally, externally, or both. Your behavior will now result from what you are thinking and feeling. If you feel good or happy, you will behave in ways that indicate goodness and happiness. If you feel bad, depressed, anxious, etc, you will behave in ways that indicate your unhappiness.

Prelude To A Paradigm Shift

What I am about to share with you is so simple, you may find it difficult to grasp and apply. What many people perceive to be complex issues that may require hours, weeks, months or years of therapy along with medication can get in the way of seeing just how simple they can resolve their own unhappiness. You may be so reluctant to accept this ensuing information because you have believed all, or most of your life, that mental illness is a disease that is the result of some chemical imbalance or some part of the brain is not functioning correctly. This has been the thinking of psychology and psychiatry since the turn of the 20th century. I will preface it by saying that what we have been doing in psychiatry for the last hundred years has been half-baked. All long-term behaviors that are being called mental illness are not illnesses at all. They have no physical pathology. Even the Diagnostic Statistical Manual for Mental Illness (DSM) admits that there are no physical laboratory findings to substantiate the existence of an illness or disease. The book correctly identifies the behaviors but labels them with names signifying a disorder or illness.

The behaviors that are being called mental illness are creative behaviors that are the result of unhappiness. They serve the purpose of easing the frustration, negative emotions, and physical ailments of not being able to control the situation as perceived. In the previous examples, and those that will follow in this book, none of the individuals are mentally ill. They are not as mentally healthy as they could be but that does not mean they are mentally ill. As you read their stories, I am sure that you would not associate their situations as being mental illness. However, if you were to observe their behavior rather than read about it, you may have a different opinion and think they have a mental illness.

While proofing this manuscript for final printing, at this very spot where you are reading, my phone rang. It was a young lady seeking counseling. I asked her what issues were causing her to want counseling and she said: "Anger

129

management, anxiety and stress, depression, improving my life, post traumatic stress, and relationship problems." She then went on to say, "I think I am seriously Bipolar and I need medication because I have been destroying my relationships."

Without realizing what she had said, she had just identified all of the causes of her unhappiness that she described..."I need medication because I have been destroying my relationships." She has fallen victim to the false world of psychiatry and the pharmaceutical companies. She believes that medication can cure her from destroying her relationships and that all of her problems are the result of a mental illness. Her unsatisfying relationships are the total cause of her unhappiness and the symptoms and behaviors for which she seeks counseling. She doesn't need a drug. She needs to understand why her choices of behaviors have not resulted in satisfying relationships and to become aware of what she has been doing to contribute to their demise.

Here Is The Key To Your Happiness

Our behavior consists of four components:
- Thinking
- Feeling
- Acting
- Physiology

We only have complete control over two of these components:

Thinking

Acting

As a result of our thinking and acting, we have *indirect* control of

Feeling (Emotions)

Physiology

We do not have direct control of these two components. However, we can indirectly control them by controlling those things in which we DO have direct control . . . our Thinking and Acting.

We always have a choice of how and what we think and how we act . . . ALWAYS.

I often hear clients say that they can't control their emotions. They are actually correct in the sense that they can't have just any emotion at will. Emotions just don't happen. They are created by whatever we are thinking about; whatever we perceive. So while we can't have direct control of our emotions, we can control what we say, think, and do that will allow them to occur and even control them. Many find it difficult to comprehend the concept that our emotions are a choice based on our thoughts.

A man calls his friend and tells him that he just scored two tickets to an NFL game this coming Sunday and invited his friend to come along. His friend thanks him for the offer but tells him, "My car isn't running very well and I need to take a look at it. If I don't get it fixed, I may not be able to make it to work Monday. Ask someone else and I'll look for you in the stands on television." So he asks several more of his male friends and because of short notice, none of them are free to go to the game with him. Feeling a bit disappointed, he accepts their refusals and doesn't make a big deal out of it. Not wanting to go to the game alone, and using his creative thinking. He has one more person to ask before giving up. . . his wife. Sure, he would rather go with a guy because it's a guy thing, in his mind. Even though she is not really into football, he asks her, "Honey, I just got two tickets to the Cardinal game. Would you go with me?" She asks, "Why don't you ask some of you friends?" He replies, "I did but they're all busy or have other plans and they can't make it." She then says, "I've never been to a pro game before and I'd like to but I have a hair appointment that took me weeks to get in with this hairdresser and I don't want to lose it." He reacts, "Damnit! You NEVER do anything I want to do!" and he storms out of the house angry.

He chose not to behave that way with his friends when they refused his offer, so why did he behave that way with his wife? He knows that if he behaved that way with his friends, they wouldn't be his friends for very long. So why behave that way with his wife? If it's okay to not do it with our friends, why do it with the people you love like your wife or kids?

He feels a sense of ownership with his family or because his wife married him and that he is the father of their children that she has an obligation to meet his needs. He feels he has a right to control her to get them to do what he wants them to do and she probably won't leave him if he does. However, if he continues to use external control on many situations, he may find that eventually, she may tire of it and she may leave him.

He didn't blow up and get upset with his friend because he didn't want to say or do anything that would harm his relationship with him. He controlled his emotions by using his thinking and his behavior. We usually don't yell or threaten the cop who pulls us over for speeding or get angry with our employer to his/her face because our thoughts tell us that doing so would cause more problems that we don't want to have. Our thinking is indirectly controlling our emotions and behavior.

Newly-weds, or recently developed love relationships, go from initial wonderful times of happiness and often end up with break-ups, separation, and divorce because they ceased using their thinking and behavior to control their emotions. In the beginning, neither partner tries to change the other person or coerce them into doing something they don't want to do.

Over time, external controlling behaviors creep into the relationship by both parties and this creates a power struggle that erodes love and respect. They go from "Just Married" . . . to "we're just married" . . . to "meet Bernie, my attorney." The use of any of the destructive, controlling power tools is the kiss of death of any relationship. They result in the loss of respect for the person who relies on them and with the loss of respect comes the loss of love. One can fall out of love as easily as they fall into it.

Refer back to the list of the seven common external controlling behaviors of criticizing, blaming, complaining, nagging, threatening, punishing, and bribing/rewarding to control. By making a conscious effort to cease using controlling behaviors in your day-to-day life, you will quickly learn to avoid them automatically or, at least, catch yourself if and when you do resort to any of them. It's truly remarkable just how happier you will be when you cease using these seven behaviors and how better your relationships with others will become.

As we go from day to day, we are always comparing what is happening around us with what we want to happen around us. We live by a series of balances or imbalances. If what we want or need to make us happy or satisfied is balanced (outside vs. inside) then we are generally happy. If what we want or need to be happy is not in balance, it is a common human trait to want to control the situation to make the two balance (outside information vs. internal wants and needs). The choices we make to balance the two will either be effective or they will fail. Those choices that are effective are filed away for future reference and use and we tend to use them often because they work for us (even if they may cause other problems).

So here is another bit of important information to aid you along the way to happiness and success:
Know what you can control and what you can't control.

The Serenity Prayer is commonly used in Alcoholics Anonymous. Here is a Choice Theory adaptation of it

> *Lord, grant me the serenity to accept the person I cannot change, the courage to change the person I can, and the wisdom to know . . . it's me.*

Since unhappiness is what we have been calling mental illness, and since unhappiness, for the most part, is the result of unsatisfying relationships with the important people in our life, we have three ways in which to find happiness by looking at the only two things we can control: Thinking and Acting.

#1. Change what you want. (Thinking)

#2. Change how behave when you don't get what you want. (Acting)

#3. Wherever possible, do *both* #1 and #2.

When someone in your life is behaving in a way in which you disapprove, the first person who needs to change is yourself.

Stop doing whatever you have been dong that has not been working. Stop trying to control the things of which you cannot control.

Change what you want, change how you act when you don't get what you want, and do both if they are applicable. There is no other way.

One can see a psychiatrist or counselor for years; take all sorts of brain medications, and nothing will overcome one's sadness and unhappy life than when they eventually end up doing any one or more of the three choices.

Looking back on your own experiences with disappointments and depression, you eventually got around to changing what you wanted and changing how you behaved after you decided you had enough of feeling bad. You recovered on your own without realizing that it was because you utilized #1, #2, or both. You didn't need psychiatric drugs or therapy to climb out of your misery. You simply chose to no longer think and behave the way you had been doing and when you made that choice, your unwanted emotions dissipated.

Simply stated, you *accepted* the reality of the given situation and realizing it is something that you cannot control but that you can control yourself. You tell yourself, 'It is what it is and now it's time to get on with my life."

Those who choose not to change their thinking and/or behaving will stay in the grips of the pharmaceutical companies and send their doctor's, therapist's or counselor's kids through college.

Change what you want.

Stop wanting something that is beyond your capability or desire to have or control . . . be it materialistic or involving another person. If you would like an expensive car that is beyond your financial capabilities, you can choose to be depressed or even angry or . . . you can find another car that you can be happy owning that is more affordable.

If you want someone to change their behavior, you probably already know that what you've been doing is not working and that you cannot control another person without harming your relationship with them. In the example of the wife who is married to the alcoholic, she cannot want her husband to be an alcoholic so she must choose the second option:

Change how you behave when you don't get what you want.

If you stop utilizing the common controlling behaviors of criticizing, blaming, complaining, nagging, threatening, punishing, or bribing/rewarding to control them or change them, you will lessen your frustration and stress. Don't be surprised if they suddenly get around to doing what you want because you quit ragging or trying to control them.

 If you stop obsessing over the other person and wanting them to change, you will find yourself functioning better and begin focusing on what you can do for yourself to be happier.

In the example of the wife who is married to the alcoholic, she must stop doing what she has been doing and begin to do something for herself. If she stops complaining, nagging, blaming, criticizing, threatening, punishing, or even bribing him to get his to stop drinking, will she have less unwanted and unhappy emotions?

If she stops behaving toward him the way she has been for several months or years, do you think he will notice? Will he become less defiant towards her demands now that she is not demanding? The answer to those questions is definitely,

"Yes." Will this, alone, cause him to stop drinking? No. It may in rare occasions but not generally. It will, however, make her life easier and less miserable.

The more you try to change someone, the more you risk harming or ending the relationship.

The next thing the alcoholic's wife could do for herself is to go to Al-anon . . . a support group for people who live with or love an addict or alcoholic. These groups consist of others who have experienced the same things, or more, than she has when it comes to her husband's drinking. There are people in these meetings who possess a lot of information and support to help her get through her situation better than anyplace else she could go . . . and it's free of cost. As stated earlier, organizations such as support groups consist of people who acquire a sense of belonging.

When dealing with others, if you stop those controlling behaviors, you may be surprised to find that the other person will start to behave differently. The change that it may bring may not be the exact change you want i.e. the alcoholic may continue to drink but you and he won't be at each other's throats over it. He will not feel pressured and you will not choose to have all of the negative emotions you have by trying to get him to stop. On the other hand, he may, indeed, decide to stop or do something about his drinking because this time, he made the decision to do so and not because his wife demanded or coerced him into doing so.

If her husband's drinking persists, she has yet another choice that is part of the "Change how you behave when you don't get what you want." She can decide to stay married and continue to walk through the wreckage his drinking creates, maintain continuous attendance with Al-Anon, or she can choose to leave him for her own mental health and wellbeing. Whatever she does will be a choice.

Ron And Maria

I got a call from Maria who informed me that she and her significant other, Ron, were having problems. She told me that it was Ron who suggested she call me personally to help her with her unhappiness. Ron had, at one time, heard a lecture I had given on Choice Theory.

Maria spent the better part of our session together telling me all about the things Ron would say or do that was causing her unhappiness. She would go on and on about Ron's behavior. She reported he had cheated on her and all they did was argue and fight about it. I found it necessary to remind Maria that Ron wasn't the person in my office seeking help and that we needed to focus on her and what she was thinking and doing that was causing her unhappiness.

This request would last for about fifteen seconds and she would go right back to talking about what Ron did. She was allowing her emotions to overpower her thinking and in so doing, had been trying to control him to make her unwanted emotions go away. To say she was emotionally distraught would be an understatement. Her current emotional state made it difficult to talk or reason with her. The more she disclosed Ron's behavior, the more emotional and agitated she would become. She was obsessing over the fact that Ron had an affair with another woman.

I asked her if she thought Ron would be willing to come see me and then afterwards we could begin seeing all of us together for future sessions. She said she believed Ron would be happy to see me because he had been impressed with my lecture on Choice Theory and that he is responsible for referring me to her. I asked her to have Ron call me for an appointment and he did.

Ron was very calm and collected when we met without Maria in attendance. In fact, his attitude was one of, "I have no problem at all. She's the one with the problem." At least Ron was willing to listen and answer questions without emotional mind blocking. He was rather cavalier in his demeanor, which, experience has taught me, could be a form of defense, and hiding behind something he didn't really want to admit.

Ron told me that he and Maria had separated a few months ago and that he had a sexual relationship with someone during that time they were separated and Maria had found out about it. Ron said he felt justified in doing so and that he had not broken any loyalty to Maria because they weren't married and had broken up. He said we were not a "committed couple" at the time. This told me that Ron was never really committed to the relationship in the first place and I began to sense that Maria was more of a convenience than a partner. So I began to seek a few more answers.

I asked, "Do you drink?" He admitted he did. I asked, "How often do you drink?" He told me he drinks every day when he comes home from work. I asked, "What do you drink and how much do you consume after work?" He said, "I have four or five beers to unwind when I get home. I only drink beer and not the hard stuff." Alcohol abusers love to say this. To them, hard liquor is what causes addiction and problems but not beer . . . that beer is just as innocuous as a soft drink. They fail to understand that there is the same amount of alcohol in a beer as there is in a shot of whiskey or a mixed drink. The only difference is that they have to consume more of the liquid to get the same amount.

I asked Ron, "What is your most favorite soft drink?" He answered, "Dr. Pepper®." I then asked him, "When was the last time you drank four or five Dr. Peppers in one sitting?" He looked at me with a sly grin and changed the subject. I had hit on something he didn't want to discuss. With all the ranting and raving Maria had expressed in my session with her, she never once brought up his drinking situation. This led me to believe that perhaps Maria had grown up in an alcoholic family where heavy and regular drinking was normal to her.

I changed the subject to ease Ron's defenses but I planned to examine the alcohol situation further down the road. Maria was five years older than Ron who was in his late forties. I asked, "Do you love Maria?" He replied that he did. I asked, "Do you want this relationship to work?" He replied that he did. I asked, "Do you plan on getting married?" He said, "Maria wants to." I said, "I was asking you not Maria. Do you want to get married?" He said, "Sure," but I wasn't convinced. After several more questions, I returned to the alcohol topic. I asked if he would be willing to complete a psychometric questionnaire about substance abuse. He was more than willing to do so. He was almost like, "Bring it on. I'll pass this thing like it's nothing."

When he had finished responding to all of the questions, the assessment returned a decision of him having a "High Probability of Having A Substance Dependence Disorder." I explained to Ron how the results were determined and that he did, indeed, have an alcohol problem. But this is not why Ron came to see me. Had I confronted his use and started to take the direction of giving him alcohol counseling, he would have left and not returned with Maria on our next planned sessions. Our session ended with him being made aware that alcohol was a problem in his life whether he believed it or not. I gave him the copy of the diagnostic results.

The next session involved both Ron and Maria. Maria, in true form, released a barrage of attacks about Ron's behavior and his "cheating" on her. Ron stood his ground and calmly explained that they had broken up at the time and that he had done no wrong in having sex with another woman during their separation.

Maria's need for power and control and wanting to change Ron were all the ingredients that lead to a relationship's demise. She kept demanding Ron admit that he had done her wrong, which Ron was not about to do. Ron's need for freedom and his addiction to alcohol is the other aspect that makes this relationship doomed unless both care enough to want to make changes in their life and relationship.

I asked Maria if Ron had been drinking every time they had a disagreement. She stated that this is usually the only time they fight. "He becomes distant, and quiet." I asked, "And how do you deal with that when he becomes distant?" Ron interrupted, "I'll tell you what she does. She nags and keeps bringing up this affair I had. She won't let it drop. I've apologized and said I'm sorry a thousand times and she won't let it go." I said to Maria, "Sounds like you won't forgive him." She said, "I can't." I said, "Yes, you can. You just don't want to. Do you think your relationship will get better if you refuse to forgive him? If you don't forgive him, how happy do you think you will be with him?"

I turned to Ron, and asked, "If every time you get into an argument you have been drinking and you guys don't argue when you haven't been drinking, what does that tell you?

I asked Maria, "Did someone in your family abuse alcohol?" She quietly said, "My father." I asked, "Do you remember the things you used to think and the emotions you used to feel when your father drank?" Maria said, "He acted just like

Ron does when he drinks." So what you are saying is that Ron's drinking seems to stir up all of your past emotions of anger when Ron drinks. Is that correct?" She said, "I never thought of it before but you're right. It makes me feel just like I did when I was a teenager and my father got drunk and they fought and argued, and he often cheated on my mother."

I asked her, "Maria, do you see how nagging and refusing to forgive Ron for his indiscretion is harming your relationship?" She admitted she did. "Ron, do you see how your drinking is causing you problems in your relationship?" He admitted he did. "So what does this tell you both what you could do to help your relationship get better?" Maria said, "Quit nagging and forgive him?" I smiled and said, "Ya think? Yes, of course. And Ron, what could you do that will help your relationship get better and stop the arguing?" He said, "Quit drinking."

"Okay. These are two things that neither of you have tried to do so far to help your relationship and bring you closer together. Are you willing to stop nagging and forgive Ron for the sake of your relationship?" Maria agreed. "Ron, are you willing to stop drinking for the sake of your relationship?" Ron agreed but I knew he was not being truthful. "Let's get back together in two weeks and see how it goes."

After two weeks they both came to see me. I asked, "How'd it go? Ron, did you remain abstinence from drinking these last two weeks?" Maria instantly jumped in and said, "He didn't even stop for one day" Ron stated, "And she started up all over again with the nagging and bringing up the past with my affair!"

I replied, "If you both agreed to me that, Maria, you would stop nagging and would forgive him, and then didn't do it, and, Ron, you agreed that you would stop drinking for two weeks and didn't, what does this tell you? It tells me that neither of you are willing to do what you said you would do for the sake of your relationship. If you aren't willing to do those things, how do you expect your conflict to work itself out? Are you waiting for some divine providence to occur that will make it all better?"

"Ron, are you willing to stop drinking for the sake of saving your relationship?" Ron said, "No." I turned to Maria and said, "So now you know where your relationship stands. Ron's drinking means more to him than having a happy relationship with you." Ron immediately jumped in, "No it doesn't! No, no, no!" Ron was trying to keep from admitting to himself that alcohol was more important to him than Maria and, at the same time, convince Maria that she mattered more. He painted himself into a corner.

I reminded him that if he couldn't stop drinking to save his relationship that there is no better indicator that his drinking is more important. I returned to Maria, "You have some new choices to make that you never considered before. You can stay in this relationship and hope it gets better on its own (it will get worse); you can go to Al-Anon to help deal with Ron's drinking and stay in the relationship; or you can end the relationship and find someone else."

It has been my experience that Maria will choose the first option and continue to be miserable until it finally gets to the point that neither one of them want to have anything to do with each other. I stated, "Neither of you are willing to put any effort to repair your damaged relationship so I don't want you to waste your money or my time so we'll end our sessions as of now."

Basically, I fired my clients. Over the years, I have learned that there is nothing that exists in a failing marriage that can't be resolved if both partners want their relationship or marriage to work and are willing to change some things they have been doing to control and change the other person. As an alcohol and drug therapist, I also know that Ron's drinking will get worse before it ever gets better. Since he refuses to do anything about his drinking, even to the point of losing his relationship, there is nothing that can be done until he sees the need.

You may notice that in all of my counseling stories with Choice Theory, I never tell clients what they have to do. In Choice Theory, the process is to define what precisely it is that the client wants; what it is that they have been doing to acquire this want; evaluate the success or failure of their attempts to get what they want; and then narrow things down so that they can see other choices on their own without being told or mandated to do anything by the counselor.

Tamara

Tamara, age 34, came to see me because she wanted to talk to a counselor. She had been diagnosed as Schizophrenic by another mental health agency and had been prescribed a common drug for that diagnosis. She came to her appointments by cab, wearing fuzzy slippers, pajamas, and a robe. Her personality was blunt . . . a flat affect. She was living at home with her parents because she could not afford her own place and was no longer working since she had so many outbursts of anger with coworkers that eventually led to her release.

The drug she had been prescribed affects multiple neurotransmitter systems and disrupts the way the brain normally functions. She had been taking the medication before she got fired from her job and some of the effects of the drug cause mood swings, anger, irritability, and fatigue. She had lost interest in the things she used to enjoy. There was no liveliness in her eyes and she had a look that would make you wonder if anyone was behind her eyes at all.

I got right to the point with her. I take it you already have a therapist otherwise you probably wouldn't be taking the medication you are on. After disclosing the name of the drug, I asked, "How many milligrams are you taking?" She told me, "ten." I continued asking, "How often do you see your therapist?" She said once a month. She said, "I only see her for about 20 minutes. We talk about how well the drug is doing and I tell her that I feel tired all the time and that I don't think the drug is helping me feel any better. In fact, I feel worse."

I asked, "What things do you talk about?" She said, "We talk mostly about how I think the medicine is working for me and if I have any side effects. She asks if I walk in my sleep, hear voices, have trouble sleeping . . . stuff like that."

I asked, "How long have you been taking your medication? She reported that she had been taking it for the last six months. I asked, "Why do you want to see me if you already have a therapist?" She stated that she thought her psychiatrist was nice but that she didn't feel like she was addressing anything that would help her . . . that all they talked about was about the medicine and if she was hearing or seeing things or wanting to hurt herself.

I asked, "What do you hope to get from coming to see me? What do you expect to get from either your psychiatrist or me?" She stated that she just wanted to feel "real" again and wanted to feel happy and be in a loving relationship. She said, "I used to see things and hear things and I don't know who it is that was talking to me or about me."

We had a few sessions with me acquiring basic information about her relationship with her parents, her sister, and even her grandmother with whom she had a close attachment. She had been a nurse's aide before being fired. I asked her if she was still seeing and hearing things and she said she wasn't since she was taking the medication. She also said that her father doesn't believe she is mentally ill but she's not so sure.

I didn't find anything unusual concerning her family relationships. She felt closer to her father than her mother but there was no obvious anger or resentment towards her. There didn't seem to be any jealousy or conflict with her older sister. Her history of relationships with the men in her life was a bit rocky. She didn't seem to have relationships that lasted very long and the men in her life usually ended the relationship with only a few exceptions.

I asked her what was going on in her life before she began seeing and hearing things and being put on medication. She told me that she had been dating an attorney who had been representing her in a legal matter and that they became involved. She almost lit up when talking about him yet there were also occasional looks and expressions of anger and sadness thrown in.

It appears that the attorney, who was acting unethically by getting involved with his client, decided he had better end the relationship. This led to Tamara's going off the deep end, so to speak. She began to stalk him and obsess about him. She called him repeatedly only to have him hang up on her. She would show up at his office wanting to see him. He finally got a restraining order against her. She developed mood swings and felt no one could understand what she felt from losing him. This is when she began to have trouble at work, got fired, and had to move back in with her parents.

Her mother was telling her to do one thing and her father was telling her to do something else and she felt caught in the middle of trying to please both of them while feeling totally rejected from the one love that she felt she could never replace. This is when she began hearing the voices. She stated they were not really audible and that they sounded like people talking far away. She said she felt that the voices were talking about her and criticizing her.

The drug she was taking has no curative abilities but it does numb the brain, keeps it from functioning normally, and has several unwanted effects that could even be life threatening.

Talking with Tamara was not all that easy. For one thing, she was on a drug that can interfere with cognition and the second problem was that she only wanted to talk about the attorney and how she could get him back in her life. At the same time, she felt revengeful and wanted to get even with him for her perception of emotionally hurting her when he ended the relationship. She had been torn between two separate emotions each of which destroyed the other. She wanted to get even with the attorney for dumping her, "I could probably cause him to lose his license" and she also wanted him back in her life. She wanted to discuss him more than herself and possible reasons that would cause him to end their relationship.   It was necessary to redirect her several times during our sessions and remind her that we were dealing with her and not the attorney.

Tamara's real problem wasn't schizophrenia. She was extremely unhappy due to having lost the love of a man with whom she had very high expectations for her future. The medication was not helping her because it stunted her mind's ability to be creative enough to work out her own resolution to her conflict. It was also hampering her cognitive ability to comprehend some of the things we talked about.

We began to discuss how effective any of her behaviors had been towards getting her what she wanted. She was slowly able to see that what she had been doing was causing the attorney to avoid her more than it was in bringing him closer to her.

During one of our sessions, her father drove her to my office and she introduced me to him. He was concerned about the medication she was taking. I gave them information about psych meds in general. I gave the reference material on the effects of these medicines and how they have never actually cured anyone. He was concerned because Tamara just wasn't the same daughter he had known all these years since she began taking the medication.

I informed him that I am not a doctor and that I cannot advise her to stop taking her medication. In fact, I strongly stated that she not stop them on her own without the supervision of a doctor. The reason for this is that when someone has been taking medication that interferes with normal brain functioning, any sudden cessation could result in some life-affecting withdrawals and severely emotional behaviors. Tamara said she didn't like how they made her feel and she didn't want to take them anymore. I suggested she talk to her psychiatrist regarding her concerns. I also informed her that her psychiatrist might suggest that they change the drug she was taking to a different drug. I also informed her that she was under no obligation to take any medication that she didn't want to take but again . . . not to stop taking the drugs unless medically supervised by either her psychiatrist or with another doctor.

Tamara asked her psychiatrist to help her stop taking the prescription she had been given. As I suspected, her doctor prescribed a different psych medication, which is often prescribed for the diagnosis of Bipolar disorder. Tamara almost instantly decided not to take and medication anymore and stopped taking them on her own without medical supervision. I had not heard from her for several weeks before she had told me that she had stopped taking them.

Common withdrawal symptoms from certain brain medications are anxiety and weight loss. Tamara lost a lot of weight over time after she had stopped taking the drug. Other withdrawal symptoms are behaviors that are often diagnosed as "bipolar," which she was later diagnosed as having. She reported not being able to concentrate, having headaches, insomnia, and feeling dizzy and depressed. Another withdrawal symptom is having suicidal ideations.

One night, while driving home from having dinner with friends, I got a call. It was Tamara. She was in tears. She told me she was in the psych ward in one of our hospitals. I was shocked. "Why?" I asked her. She said, "I took a lot of sleeping pills." Again I asked, incredulously, "Why in the world would you do that?" As soon as I asked that question, I was instantly reminded of the drugs she had been taking. Suicidal ideations are part of the warnings of taking the medications she had been given. Her answer to my question was even more astounding. She said, "I was really, really tired and I needed to get to sleep."

It was here that I dropped my client/counselor manner with her. She had gotten to know and trust me well enough over the last few months so I felt okay in coming across to her in a stern voice. I said, "Tamara, don't give me that lame-assed excuse. Why did you really overdose?" She didn't answer. Instead, she said, "can you get me out of the hospital?" I said, "Not a chance in hell. Your choice to overdose is why you are there and I can do nothing to get you out even if I wanted to. You're there until they deem you are no longer a threat to yourself."

Tamara hung up and I didn't hear from her again for several months. She had now been prescribed another psych med used as a mood stabilizer for bipolar and depression. She called for an appointment and I asked her what had been going on in her life that she decided to overdose. She had quit taking her medication on her own with no medical supervision and began to obsess once again about the lawyer. She stated she met with him with the hope that he would have a change of heart and renew their relationship. She reported that he was not interested in doing so and told her to forget about him and get on with her life.

I could see where this was going. She had tried everything that she knew to get him back and to no avail. She began to use her creativity and came up with the idea that if she made an attempt to commit suicide, that he would feel guilty and see just how much he meant to her and would reconsider their relationship.

She made an appointment. As I had surmised, during our session I discovered that she did exactly as I thought. Her suicidal plan was to get attention. It may also have been the result of her drug withdrawal. She had a plan that would keep her from actually taking her life. She called a friend and told her she was suicidal and was going to take her life. The friend then called 9-1-1 and her parents.

She asked me, 'Am I crazy?" I said, "YES!" You aren't really crazy but your behavior certainly is. You're trying to control something that you can't control and this is part and parcel of why you used to hear voices and were paranoid, along with some other things that we talked about in past sessions. Your frustration and failure to get what you want in life is consuming your thoughts to act in any way you can come up with that makes sense to you at the time you think of it. When you decided to take all of those pills, it made perfect sense to you because you visualized that it would help you get him back by proving how much you loved him. You even went so far as to plan your rescue by calling your friend and telling her what you were going to do. It all made sense to you at the time. So tell me. How did you enjoy the charcoal lavage?" Tamara made a face indicating her disgust and said, "Never again."

"So now, looking back on what you chose to do . . . was it worth it? Did it help get him back or drive him further away?" She replied, "He won't even take my calls." I said, "It looks like everything you have been doing to make this man love you aren't working. Is that right?" She agreed. "So why continue to do things that don't work." She replied, "If I keep trying, maybe something *will* work."

The story continues but to move along, I will report that Tamara eventually found a more sympathetic doctor to wean her off of her meds while she continued to see me. I began to see the true person she was meant to be as indicated by a sparkle in her eyes and being more energetic.

How did Tamara finally find a better life? By applying the principles of Choice Theory, she realized that she could not get someone to do something they didn't want to do. She learned that what she had been doing was not effective and she needed to make better choices of behavior. What really gave her an epiphany was that she had to accept the reality of the situation that the relationship she so badly wanted with the attorney was not going to happen and that she needed to quit trying to make it happen. From this, she learned that when someone in her life was not behaving the way that she wanted him or her to behave . . . she had to be the person to change.

 Having learned Choice Theory and how to apply it, she eventually turned her life around. She gained employment and got her own place. She is enjoying her own company now and reports, "I'm spending my time getting to know me better so that I can have better relationships. I see that if I want to have a healthy relationship, I need to be a healthier person." Tamara is doing well and not on medication. She has several friends of both gender but not in any romantic relationship at this time. Her parents no longer are telling her what they think she needs to do because she has found her own way to happiness and a better life.

She no longer hears voices and is enjoying life more than she has in the past. She states her greatest learning experience comes from knowing that she can only control herself and that she always has a choice in how she thinks and behaves . . . and that she can control her emotions based upon controlling her thinking and behavior.

As Henry Higgins exclaimed, "By Jove, I think she's got it!"

In Tamara's case, she was trying to control something of which she had no control. It's easy to find someone to love. Finding someone to love us in return is not so easy. We can't make others love us.

Tamara was also torn between trying to satisfy her parent's directives. Each of them had different ideas of what they wanted her to do with her life. She didn't want to disappoint either of them but she also didn't want to do what either of them wanted her to do. This often leads to some very frustrating and difficult decisions that she felt guilty if she didn't do them. Mix the emotion of guilt along with shame and low self worth and one will find many a person who has been diagnosed as schizophrenic.

Tamara felt her total life was out of control; that others were controlling her, and she was attempting to make some sort of sense out of it. The muffled voices she reported hearing were the result of guilty feelings of not being able to please her parents who were always telling her what she should do. She also felt that people were criticizing her behind her back as being someone who was inept and mentally ill. She couldn't hear the voices clearly because she felt she knew what they were saying and she didn't want to hear it.

Right now, I know there are some readers who might say, "But hearing voices isn't normal. That's got to be mental illness." Have you ever heard a song or have a song come to your mind and you sing it in your mind for hours on end as if you can't get it out of your head? If you are like most mentally healthy people, you have had this experience. So when you experienced this, were you mentally ill? You may even have said to yourself, "This song is driving me crazy. I can't get it out of my head." This is no different than the person who hears voices. Voices, thoughts, and songs can be played over and over in the mind almost to the point that you may feel that you actually are going crazy.

Voices can be the response of having to make severe decisions on something when the person doesn't like any of the choices they have to decide. Constant criticism and even discrimination can contribute to hearing voices as well as experiencing any trauma. Seeking external answers to ease the frustration and anguish of making difficult choices to resolve a problem can lead to the brain's ability to create and hear voices.

Tamara's behavior was intended to change the image she perceived of a failed relationship to match the image she had in her Quality World of a happy relationship with an attorney and they would live happily ever after. She was desperately trying to satisfy her love and belonging needs as well as her power needs. If one behavior didn't satisfy her need, she would create other possible behavior to satisfy them.

Once again: ***All we do from birth until death is behave. And all behavior is chosen to satisfy happiness or pleasure and to satisfy one or more of our basic genetic needs of survival, love and belonging, power, freedom, and fun***.

Anxiety

When helping clients attain the happiness they wish to acquire, I can only approach their ability to deal with the things that they have the ability to control . . . their thinking and behavior in more satisfying ways. Telling someone to "cheer up" or "pull yourself up by the boot straps" is empty rhetoric that will have no effect when a person does not understand that they have two specific choices that they can control. Since a client doesn't have the ability to directly control their physiology or their emotions, a therapist or counselor would have even less ability to do so with a client.

Anxiety is a very common condition that plagues many people for many different reasons. It seems to always be rooted in fear and frustration when nothing seems to be working to resolve an unhappy situation. Much of it is the result of "what ifs." What if this will happen? What if that will happen? Depending on the situation, one might also feel lost for answers to making their life better that they become extremely frustrated for not knowing what to do after everything else they have done has not been successful. Anxiety is the result of what a person perceives at the time of their anxiety episode, which includes another person(s) or themselves.

It is not uncommon for many people to suffer from "stage fright" or public speaking. Their anxiety is the fear of the what if's. "What if I say something they will disagree with," or "What if I am wrong?" "What if I am challenged?" "What if people don't like me or how I look?" or "What if they can see my shortcomings?" The thought of many eyes looking only at you can be a scary thought for those who lack confidence in themselves or their presentation. As a public speaker, I often feel a bit anxious speaking before groups of people. I have learned to use this emotion as a way to keep me alert about what I want to say. I still have the what ifs when I speak in the order of, "What if I forget to say this or that?" I eventually come to realization that my audience has no idea what I may have omitted to say so why worry? I also have come to realize that I soon overcome my anxiety of speaking before large groups of people after a few minutes into the lecture.

But there are numerous situations that can be more anxious than public speaking. In most cases, the anxiety will involve someone else in the sufferer's life. It can be someone's health, someone's behavior, someone else's problem that the sufferer has become involved, a life or death situation, or the fear that others will "discover" something about them that they don't want to be known.

Alan and Anxiety

If Alan, the son of an associate I mentioned in a previous chapter, was to seek counseling from me, I would do more to pay attention to his accomplishments and abilities as a capable person more than his symptoms of anxiety (fears). He may want to talk about his physical discomfort and unwanted emotions and how they affect him when he panics or feels anxiety. I will acknowledge those points but only to reassure him that I understand he feels that way. Again . . . knowing how or why someone feels or does the things they do will not necessarily bring about any change unless something is done to stop the unwanted feelings. Since he can only directly control this thinking and behavior, there is little need to spend focusing on any and all of his unhappy feelings.

Alan's situation involves his mother, stepfather, the mother of his children, and himself, and people in general. That's quite a load for anyone to carry. Look at all the people in his life that he feels he has difficulty. He has leaned that drugs and alcohol were the only thing he could rely on to deal with unwanted emotions. If he were actively drinking or using, that would be the first order of business. But currently, he no longer appears to be relying on this method to allay his unhappiness.

He begins to have an anxiety attack when he is in the midst of a lot of other people in a crowd.   Usually, the onset of an anxiety attack occurs when he is having difficulty with other people and begins to feel fearful. To ward off his anxiety, he lashes out to them with the intent of putting them on the defensive side. He also has deep fear of being "found out" as being incompetent and unskilled in areas of which he has no confidence or even knowledge. His anxiety is what has been affecting his social skills and relationships, as well as keeping him from being employed. Alan is not a happy person by any stretch of the imagination.

If he were a client of mine, I would want to discover what Alan really wants in his life that he could get if he were to change the way he thinks and behaves. What are the things that he can change?   I can't ask him to merely stop panicking or feeling anxious, or feeling physically uncomfortable. Those things can only be stopped by the things he thinks and does. Continuing to do the things he enjoys doing, and does well, will be an asset and encouraged.

Alan would be a difficult client because as a therapist, he would fear that I would "discover" all of his unwanted perceptions of himself. He would, most likely, want to fight and argue with me on any given area to keep me from discovering too much about him. Careful choices of words and concepts on my part would be necessary. The last thing he needs to hear from me would be that he is choosing to feel anxious and any of his other emotions that have been causing him unhappiness. Should the situation present itself where he does blow up in anger to precede any feeling of anxiety, I would not try to stop him. Nor would I allow his behavior to have any effect on me and would watch calmly without trying to calm him down.

Once he would calm down on his own, I would ask him if what he just said and did made his life better at getting what he wants in life or did it possibly have a way of keeping him from getting what he wants. I would ask if his behavior brought us closer together as someone who is helping him or did it possibly drive me away? If he is trying to put me on the defensive and back off, I won't go there. I will remind him that the only person in the room who is unhappy and feeling angry and miserable is him. Then I would ask if he thinks that what he just displayed helps him connect with others or drive them away from him. Alan's verbal attacks on others is his way of controlling his anxiety and it has been working for him to avoid the anxiety but causing him all of his other problems of unhappiness.

The next concern would be to address his relationship with his mother and stepfather. He is holding a lot of resentment and anger over past events that he is not willing to dispel. He finds his anger about past events gives him power and strength that he holds over them when he begins to feel powerless and misunderstood. If he didn't lash out, he would feel deeper frustration and work himself into a panic attack and feel out of control.

Again, I would not want to discuss the events of the past for the obvious reasons that the past cannot be changed. What can change, however, are his thoughts and behavior concerning the past. I would want him to describe to me how he would like his relationship with his mother and stepfather to be that would cause him to feel happy and not angry. Then we would explore the things that he might do differently that would lead to the results that he would prefer to have. He may want to say that they need to change or do something but I would remind him that the only people we can control is ourselves, not others. What can he do for the sake of their relationship and not for the sake of the individuals? Once he begins to think and behave differently, he will find that his mother and stepfather will automatically begin to behave differently towards him.

Taking one step at a time, Alan's next area of concern would be applying his new-learned skills with others in his social life as well as exploring what he might do to improve his financial earnings and responsibilities. Doing so would result in acquiring self-confidence and self-esteem. When put together, Alan would find less and less reasons for choosing behaviors that would lead to any anxiety attacks. There's more to address Alan's situation than I mention here but his story allows me to explain how he can control his unhappiness and anxiety by controlling the only two things that he can control . . . his thinking and behaving.

As Good As It Gets

Once again, I reference the film industry. In the movie, "As Good As It Gets," Jack Nicholson portrays the character Melvin Udall. Helen Hunt portrays the waitress Carol Connelly, and Greg Kinnear as Simon Bishop, the gay artist who has been robbed and severely beaten.

Melvin Udall is a romantic book novelist with some serious personality defects. He pushes people away by being rude, demanding, and angry. Most any psychiatrist would diagnose him as Bipolar with an Avoidant Personality Disorder, as well as Obsessive/Compulsive. He can't deal with things that are not perfectly aligned. He washes his hands with separate small bars of soap for each washing, never using the same bar of soap again. He brings his own eating utensils to the restaurant that he goes to each morning for breakfast and orders the same breakfast. He insists of eating at the same table each time he has breakfast and should anyone be sitting at his table when he gets there, he will insult them until they leave. Only one waitress in the restaurant tolerates him and is willing to wait on him. He refuses to step on any crack on sidewalks or on tiled floors that have defined borderlines. This is not a man most people would like to know much less be around. Both professionals and laypersons would also call him "mentally ill".

The gay artist, Simon, has been brutally beaten in a robbery of his home and finds it necessary to find someone to care for his pet dog, Verdell. The only available person on the same apartment floor as Simon is Melvin who refuses to care for the dog but is taken in after being threatened by Simon's agent.

One morning, Melvin's waitress, Carol, does not show up for work to wait on him because she has a son who suffers from asthma. Melvin, finds out where she lives and arranges for his personal doctor to go to her home and give Carol's son special attention that she never found with any other doctors her son had been seeing. Melvin's intentions are not out of the goodness and kindness of his heart, or the concern for her son, but rather to insure that she would not miss work anymore and would be available to take his breakfast order each morning.

Meanwhile, Simon's dog, Verdell, began to reach the softer side of Melvin. Melvin begins to connect with him by seeing to his needs. Verdell also begins to connect with Melvin as they were both reluctant to connect with each other at first. Carol is beginning to see the softer side of Melvin, albeit only slightly. But even *slightly* is a lot of change for Melvin. Carol has also lightened up on her attitude towards Melvin because of his arrangements he made with the doctor for her son.

Simon finds it necessary to drive to his parent's home to seek financial support as he is about to lose everything due to medical bills and loss of income after being attacked. Simon's father had disowned him for being gay and threw him out of the house several years ago and this was making the trip to ask for financial support all the more difficult. Simon asked Melvin to drive him back East and Melvin saw this as a possible way to get close to Carol. (Melvin was beginning to react to the need for love and belonging as a result of Verdell's eventually connecting him with his long-lost affectionate side). Melvin agrees to drive Simon if Carol would agree to go along with them on the trip. She accepts. Once they arrive, Melvin finds the courage to ask Carol out for a date. She agrees to go with him for dinner. The restaurant host would not allow Melvin in the restaurant without a sport coat, or suit and tie. Melvin recalls seeing a nearby clothing store along the way so he asks Carol to wait for him while he goes to get the apparel. The store has tiled floors so Melvin refuses to enter. Instead, he stands in the doorway and points to the clothing and tie racks and tells the salesman, "I'll take that coat and that tie." He then returns to the restaurant where Carol is having a drink while waiting for his return.

Melvin begins to admire her at the bar from afar before she notices his presence. His genetic basic need for love and belonging is kicking in. He meets her at the bar and, in true Melvin fashion, says something that sets her relationship with him backwards. He says, "They refuse to let me come in without a coat and tie and yet they let you to come in wearing a simple house dress."

Having been insulted, Carol becomes indignant and demands he pay her a compliment or their date is over before it even starts. Melvin stutters and stammers and says he needs some time to come up with one and by the time they get to their table he will have a complement for her. They get seated and Carol says, "Well? I'm waiting."

Here is where Choice Theory and Dr. Glasser's concept that "all long term emotional problems are relationship problems" comes into play and that we have certain needs that make up our happiness (or lack of them). In this example, the need is for love and belonging and acceptance.

Melvin says, "You make me want to be a better man."
Carol replies, "That is probably the nicest thing anyone has ever said to me."

Melvin had developed all of his unsavory behaviors as a means of survival and power to gain some form of control in his life when he felt he had none. His current antisocial and compulsive behavior was something that gave him a sense of being in control. Actually, Helen didn't "make" him want to be a better man. He realized that if he wanted to have a meaningful relationship with her, he would have to change.

One might ask, "what about the obsessive behavior? Isn't that mental illness? Normal people don't do that." You would be correct. "Normal" people don't do that as a rule. But normal people do similar things when they don't wish to be reminded or think of unwanted thoughts and emotions or feel they have no control of other things in their life.

Remember when you were a child and when someone would be saying things to you that you didn't want to hear? You probably plugged up your ears and sang syllables of an indistinct tune, "la, la, la, la, etc."

Melvin, and others, who don't want to be reminded or think of unwanted things, compensate for it by doing something that distracts or disrupt their thinking and it eventually becomes a habit. Repeated behaviors allowed for the ability to be able to control what one doesn't want to hear or think about in their own head.

Melvin realizes that if he is to have any sort of meaningful relationship with someone, he has to make some changes in his behavior and what he has been doing has not been working. He is now finding that he has needs for love and belonging that won't get met unless he changes his behavior. He then begins to attempt to walk normally and soften up on his demands and rudeness as they make a go at a relationship.

In real life, this relationship is still doomed because Melvin is not about to make a total hundred and eighty degree turn overnight. It will take some time for Melvin to make the necessary changes he will experience with others. But the story makes for a nice happy ending as they walk hand in hand although Melvin is walking on the curb and not the sidewalk.

Chapter 9 - Money, Power, and Fame Mean Nothing Without Meaningful Relationships

Howard Hughes was at one time, the most financially successful man in America. He inherited his money from his

father who was the owner of the Hughes Tool Company. His father invented a tri-bit rock drill bit during the Texas Oil Boom era. Howard Sr. died at age fifty-four and left seventy-five percent of his business to Howard, Jr.. The other twenty-five percent was willed to Senior's parents and brother. Howard, at age 19, bought out his grandparents and uncle and now owned one hundred percent of the tool company. Howard then hired someone to run his company while he pursued other interests . . . namely aviation and filmmaking. It's interesting to note that Howard's grandmother, aunts and uncle all had background in the arts of opera and concert singing and novel and screenplay writing.

Howard became successful in many business ventures involving films, aviation, movie theaters, real estate, and radio stations. He was a scratch golfer but eventually gave it up to focus on other financially rewarding ventures. He survived four aircraft crashes that left him with aches and pains that would plague him throughout his life. With all of his successes, there was one thing he could never hold onto . . . his romantic relationships . . . and later, all other social and business relationships. Here was a man whom you might think had the world by the tail: Money, success, recognition, admirers, excitement, movie stars, cars, planes, and women who wanted to be with him.

Howard had married in 1925 and he and his wife moved to California to begin all of his movie and aviation pursuits. His wife, Ella, filed for divorce in 1929. He dated many of the most famous movie actresses of the time. His obsessive business concerns kept him from being able to meet the needs of any serious long-lasting relationship. Movie actress Gene Tierney said, "I don't think Howard could love anything that did not have a motor in it." He married Jean Peters in 1957 but she was more focused on her career than marriage. Howard had her followed everywhere she went. He had listening devices throughout the home and phone. He threatened to ruin the career of Gene Peter's co-star if he didn't leave her alone.

Howard was a man who tried to control everything in his life including his relationships. The two women that he seemed to be interested in the most were Ava Gardner and Katherine Hepburn. Both of these women were strong women who were not intimidated by his wealth and success. He couldn't control them and as a personal observation, I wonder if he actually admired their courage and strength, or if they were a challenge he felt compelled to overpower.

While staying at the Desert Inn in Las Vegas and taking over a complete level of floors for several weeks, he was eventually asked to check out of the hotel so that they could rent the rooms out to other people. Instead of leaving, he bought the hotel. He then began to buy up several Las Vegas properties and began to isolate and exhibit eccentric behavior. He would talk to people who came to see him without opening the door to his hotel suite. Even those he trusted were not allowed entry.

He would obsess over the size of vegetable peas insisting they all be the same size on his plate. Film director, Richard Fleischer, wrote in his autobiography, *Just Tell Me When to Cry*, about the difficulty in dealing with Hughes. He wrote that Hughes was often so involved with trivial details (obsessing) that he was often indecisive and was also very stubborn. His dealing with Hughes on films caused concern that their work would never be completed due to Hughes' unpredictable mood swings.

In one instance of his dating, he came to find out that one of the women he had dated had contracted a sexually transmitted disease. He began to distrust women and avoided sexual contact. He became a germaphobe and began to develop aversions to anything that might have contaminants of any sort from anyone. He locked himself in his Desert Inn room and refused to see anyone including some of the women whom he did trust. He would sign necessary business documents by having them put in a basket with a rope tied to them and then hauled up to his office window and after signing them, would return them in the same manner. Passing documents under the door was also a utilized method. He would repeat things to himself over and over concerning the most trivial matters on how to do something and even write instructions on the methods to be applied when doing them. He amassed several bottles of his urine and lined them up in his room.

You would most likely think that here was a man on the verge, if not already, of insanity. But he could control his earlier peculiar behaviors when he had to. Before he became a total recluse, He was brought up before the

Senate committee for wasted war spending of government money brought about from Maine Senator, Owen Brewster. The conflict between the two was rooted in Brewster's connection with the owner of Pan Am airlines, Juan Trippe, who was intending to have a monopoly on world-wide air travel and keep Hughes's company, Trans World Airlines (TWA), from having the same right. Brewster and Juan Trippe were in collusion to buy out Howard's TWA Company so that they could gather the sole market for international air travel.

After Howard exposed unethical business practices of Owen Brewster during the senate hearings, the charges against Hughes were dismissed as the hearing committee determined that both Hughes' and Brewster's questionable business practices cancelled each other out.

It was after these hearings on national television that Hughes decided that he was never going to allow himself to be the center of attention again or be exposed to the national public. He began to increase his penchant for isolation and privacy.

Howard's fame, money, and business ventures consumed his life to the point that he obsessed over everything while never developing adequate social skills to deal with others especially those of any loving and meaningful relationships. He had more than enough money for survival, which also afforded his need for power, acceptance, and achieving. He also used his power to control other people and the women in his life, which is why he had so much difficulty with them. He had not learned how and when to turn on and off his power motivators and with whom to use them to achieve his desired wants.

His freedom and fun were both one and the same . . . flying. He truly loved it and was fascinated by it. Not only did he love to fly, he loved to create the largest and fastest planes that could be invented at the time.

He had everything he ever wanted at his fingertips except for what he wanted, but could never seem to acquire . . . love and belonging. His mind was so filled with minute details that they would overpower his thinking and he would obsess on any one or more to gain a sense of being in control.

Of all the five basic motivation needs, I contend that once you have acquired the need for Love and Belonging, that all the other needs of survival, power, freedom, and fun will come more easily.

Take a moment to reflect upon your own life. Recall any of the times you felt you had found the person in your life that you loved and who loved you in return. What was your life like at that time? Not only were you, most likely, very happy, you also had more energy to do other things that provided your other basic needs.

You may also reflect on a time when you had lost the love of your life. While there are those who possess a fairly good balance of emotions, there are others who may have experienced isolation, moodiness, severe depression, loss of appetite, loss of sleep, loss of concentration, and hours and hours of obsessing over the love that was lost. Nothing of any past importance may seem to have held any importance at all after your loss. You may have lost several pounds from loss of appetite or gained a lot of weight to comfort yourself with food.   Alcohol and drugs are common behaviors people choose to deal with their unhappiness. These choices of behavior can also be found with those who have lost a love due to death.

The loss of love, for whatever reason, can lead to grief and depressive behaviors to deal with the loss. Only when the reality of the situation and accepting it does the grief and sadness end and life moves on.

When Howard Hughes died, he was six feet and four inches tall and weighed only 90 pounds. He had five broken hypodermic needles in his arm from injecting codeine. He died from malnutrition and kidney complication. All other organs, including his brain, were deemed perfectly healthy. He had stopped taking care of his appearance long ago and had long hair and beard. His toenails and fingernails had grown long and not manicured. His hirsute looks made him unrecognizable as the famous and wealthy businessman everyone could identify. He had to be fingerprinted to correctly identify him as he no longer looked like any of his photos or past resemblances.

The Drug Makers Big Lie

In the 1995 movie, "The Usual Suspects, " Roger "Verbal" Kint, says the line, "The greatest trick the devil ever pulled was convincing the world he didn't exist."

The greatest trick the pharmaceutical companies ever pulled was convincing the world that depression is the result of a chemical imbalance. The claim is that depression is caused by a lack of serotonin. So they created a drug that stops the brain from doing its normal functioning of a Serotonin uptake and keeps the neurotransmitter, serotonin, actively present the brain.

So if you use that sort of reasoning, the main cause of getting a headache is because you don't have enough aspirin in your brain. Totally ridiculous.

There is no way that the chemicals in one's brain can be measured. The brain would have to be removed, ground up in a food processor, then all the liquid would have to be removed. Following that procedure, the different liquids that would be extracted would have to be separated and then . . . what is considered to be "normal" levels?

"If any chemical imbalance exists in your brain, a doctor put it there." Dr. Peter Breggin

Dr. Breggin further states that "psychiatric drugs don't correct biochemical imbalances . . . they cause them. Psychiatric drugs are developed precisely with the aim of causing biochemical imbalances in the normal brain."[1]

I often hear people say, "My life was a mess before I started taking my meds. They made me feel better and function better." As an alcohol and drug therapist, I can assure you that both alcohol and illicit drugs make people feel better too.

____

[1] Breggin, Peter, MD, Medication Madness, St. Martin Press, NY p. 270

That's why they use them. But none of them have ever corrected their so-called mental disorder. In fact, they caused more problems. The same applies to psych meds. Just because you may feel better and act differently doesn't mean you have been cured of any disorder or illness.

"No psychiatric drug is known to correct anything in the brain." Peter Breggin, MD

Pharmaceutical companies devised the chemical imbalance concept and sold it not only to the public by way of television and other media, but also convinced several doctors that their lie was actually the cause of depression. Why? Of course . . . to sell the antidepressant drugs. The number of prescriptions for antidepressant drugs, Select Serotonin Reuptake Inhibitors (SSRIs), more than tripled after they made this false announcement. And when sales began to slump, the pharmaceutical companies declared that it also works for other things like anxiety, Bipolar, and obsessive-compulsive behavior and sales began to increase once again.

Big Pharma has made billions of dollars by drugging people's minds with chemicals that stop the uptake of the "feel good" neurotransmitter, Serotonin. With the buildup of Serotonin, the brain fails to function as it is designed to normally function and emotions are compromised. There is no single drug that can have any effect on any one emotion. These medications affect all emotions, not just the emotion of unhappiness. Once you change the way your brain works, it doesn't easily, if at all, return to the way it is supposed to work.

Studies have shown that a placebo works just as well and even better in many cases, as an antidepressant.[2] This begs the question, how many of the antidepressants were actually the result of the placebo effect? Antidepressants and other brain medications inhibit the mind's ability to create and it is our creativity that allows us to resolve our own unhappiness.

---

[2] Sited March 14, 2018:
https://www.madinamerica.com/2018/03/new-study-concludes-antidepressants-largely-ineffective-potentially-harmful/
https://www.webmd.com/mental-health/news/20080227/antidepressants-no-better-than-placebo

> **Important Warning:**
>
> **Once prescribed and taking psychiatric drugs, no one should stop taking them or cut down on their usage without a doctor's medical or clinical supervision. Doing otherwise may result in serious withdrawal symptoms and even life-threatening emotional reactions.**

We all experience sadness many times in our lives and every experience involves the loss of someone due to breakups and divorce, death, or disappointment of something that was wanted or expected, but not acquired or realized. There are also many types of natural disasters that involve loss and result in sadness but, by far, the most common causes of sadness is the death of a loved one and the end of a relationship or divorce. In simple terms, we have lost a relationship with someone important to us or we were involved in an unsatisfying relationship. In more direct terms, "someone important to us is not behaving the way we want them to behave.

What may be surprising for some people to see is that our sadness is very self-centered. We feel sorry for ourselves and for what we no longer have. To feel sad over the death of someone close to us is a natural human emotion. If someone we don't care for or someone with whom resentment may exist dies, sadness may not be something that one experiences. It is not perceived as a personal loss and it occurred to someone not very important to us.

I recall the longtime feud between Bette Davis and Joan Crawford. When Crawford died, Davis is known to have said, "I was brought up to always say good things about anyone who died. Joan Crawford is dead. Good."

There is no set time for someone to begin to stop depressing. It ends when one becomes tired of feeling bad enough to realize that they have a choice on how they feel and change their thinking and behavior. Long term suffering and the inability to function well combined with adverse effects on relationships with others is not something emotionally, or even physically, healthy regardless of the length of time it lasts. Unfortunately, the general form of treatment, even for simple sadness, is for doctors to prescribe medications that only keep the brain from functioning normally. Even some of these medications have been known to cause suicidal thoughts and behaviors.

Those who have yet to understand the concepts of Choice Theory may mistake them to mean that all one has to do is "buck up . . . pull yourself up by your bootstraps" and get on with your life. That is not Choice Theory. Choice Theory is realizing that we have direct control of two things that create our emotions and affect our physiology and those two things are our Thoughts and our Behavior.

Obsessive thinking, both conscious and those just below our level of consciousness, are debilitating and fuel the sadness and emotions associated with the perceptions of personal losses, emotional wounds, betrayals, abandonments, and resentments. They are the things that keep one stuck in a world of misery and create the perception of being totally helpless to do anything about their situation. Those who have overcome their past depression will tell you that what changed it for them was relinquishing their attempts to control their situation, *accept* the reality of the situation; *stop trying to change someone* or hoping the behavior of someone else will change; identifying what they would rather have in life than what they have been experiencing; evaluating how all they have been doing by depressing has only made their situation worse or added to their frustration; and performing new behaviors.

Excluding natural disasters, when was the last time you felt sad or depressed when it didn't involve someone else? I would be very surprised if you could.

Suicide is the ultimate result of sadness and feeling helpless. Some antidepressant medications, supposedly designed to deal with depression, have black box warnings that the medication has the possibility of causing suicidal thoughts or behaviors. You would think that some people taking these medications for depression would see the insanity of taking a medication that would cause worse depressing. The rationale for taking these medications is generally, "Well, a doctor prescribed it so it must be safe." Others may risk the dangers as long as they can stop feeling as badly as they do.

The use of Illegal drugs and alcohol to deal with one's unhappiness is yet another way to self-medicate for unwanted emotions, shame and guilt. Alcohol dependence has been called a slow suicide.

As a person who has experienced several bouts of severe depression, I feel quite qualified to be able to share my thoughts and understanding of depression. Since being educated and trained in Choice Theory and having experienced ultimate betrayal, deaths, and loss of love since acquiring this knowledge, I can tell you that while these events were unhappy circumstances, they were not debilitating or the cause of any deep depression as they had been in the past.   To put it in its most simple terms, the following thoughts and self-talk is your guide to resolving your unhappiness:

- Whatever happened has happened. It's called "Life."
- Whatever happened is out of my control so "let it be."
- Whatever happened is the result of what others feel they need to do to get their needs met so leave them alone to find their own happiness. I need to do whatever I have to do to get my own needs met.
- I deserve to be happy and successful and my thoughts about the person(s) or situation are the major cause that is preventing me from having happiness and success. I will change my thinking and/or divorce myself from toxic people.
- I realize that choosing to feel miserable, both emotionally and physically, is not helping me get what I need to be happy and successful..
- I'll say "yes" to opportunities that I would usually avoid or those things I always had an alibi for not doing. I'll kick-start my positive feelings by accomplishing things.
- I'll do things for myself for a while instead of for others. I can help others best by being better myself.

An inexperienced pilot finding himself in a storm may fly all around the storm clouds looking for a way out and in so doing . . . run out of fuel and crash. The experienced pilot will continue his course knowing that he will eventually come safely out on the other side of the storm.

Our emotions are the music of our soul. What type and tone of music describes you soul?

Control your thinking and/or your behavior to overcome depression. There is no other way.

So what causes depression? Let's go back to the previous chapter where we perceive information (an object, place, situation, or occurrence) that occurs outside of our physical being and we compare it to the images in our brain's Quality World of those things that we value, things that we like, or things that we want or believe they should be that will make us happy. If the perception outside ourselves does not match the image in our Quality World, we experience some sort of glitch and it throws our homeostasis off. We tell ourselves, "something is happening (or happened) that is not what I want and I need to do something that will match my Quality World image."

So we begin to do something to "fix" it and make it match. If we run out of the ways we rely on to fix things, we invent new ways to make it match. The more things that don't work, the more we become frustrated and unhappy. Many people would stop at this point in trying to fix it and choose to depress. Others may go off the deep end and choose some extreme behaviors to try and fix it or, at least, do something that will ease their unhappiness and frustration. By extreme, I mean such behaviors as mass shooting, murder, violence, suicide, stalking, anorexia/bulimia, alcohol and drugs, anxiety, obsessive/compulsive thinking and behaving, hearing voices, etc., etc.

When I tell clients that they are choosing to depress, they look at me like I'm the crazy one. They begin to have second thoughts about coming to see me for their unhappiness. I then explain that depression is a choice . . . a way to deal with something that they feel is out of their control to fix or do anything about. It makes one feel that there is something they could do but, for the life of them, they don't know what that something is or they don't want to do it. They have an option to either get angry or stuff their anger. They would prefer not to be angry so they control their anger by turning their anger inwardly.

That is one reason why people choose to depress. It keeps their anger in check and from lashing out or possibly doing harm to self or others. It is impossible to be angry and depressed at the same time. One or the other emotion will overcome the other. Just ask any person who may have struck out against another person. "Were you sad when you did what you did or were you angry?"

Another reason why people choose to depress is to get help from others without having to come out and directly ask for it. Have you ever seen someone who is choosing to depress? You can see it in their facial expression, their body language, their tone of voice, and the things they may say. If so, you may have approached them and asked, "Are you okay?" They just got help without asking you for it.

Others may feign depression along with their actual bouts of unhappiness as a tool to manipulate others. Since depressing resulted in getting help and attention from others when the depression was real, why not use it to get attention when you feel lonely and have no friends or want someone to do something for you? Depressing can become a tool to manipulate or control others by playing on the sympathy and concern from others.

My mother was a masterful professional depressor. She had a history of growing up with a lot of family shame and guilt and traumatic events that she carried all her life. Whenever anything occurred that would cause her to feel unhappy or get someone to behave to her liking, she would switch on the depression button, get quiet, wear a very sad expression, speak in a sad tone of voice when spoken to, or even not talk at all and could do this for days and even months.

She had some very good reasons to depress in the past but she never did anything to put them behind her and move on with her life. She was from that generation that believed that one should not talk about shameful events and unhappiness. She learned over the years that depressing could be a very effective way to control the behavior of others, specifically her family. She would rely on it often. The family would always go out of their way to "try and make Mom happy."

Depressing To Control Others

I was part of that cast of players until I recognized what was happening. After I completed my education, she learned that her depressing role no longer had any controlling effect on me. She used her creativity to develop another behavior to get attention and control me. Her tactic would be to go to the other family members who were still endlessly tying to

"Make Mother happy," and would tell them things that would cause them to choose to resent me . . . things that were false or did not occur. This would turn them against me and make me the villain. It got her the attention she wanted as she had no friends, having pushed them all out of her life, and was a widow. Her four children were the only people she maintained in her life and three of them lived in other States.

When some people realize that they cannot control another person, they often will try to control how others will react to the person they can't control. This is a form of triangulation ...bringing others into the manipulation scenario to get the other person to behave the way they want them to behave. They may rely on criticizing, blaming, complaining, and making false claims about the person they can no longer control. Then, the others get involved out of anger and resentment and gang up on the innocent person to force him/her to be compliant and obedient.

Reasons Why People Choose To Depress

People choose to depress, and/or act like they are depressed, for the following reasons:

    1.   A tool used to control others.

    2.   A way to get attention when lonely

3.	A way to get help without having to ask for it.

4.	A way to keep their anger under control

There is yet another reason people choose to depress and one that I find very common:

5.	The reluctance or refusal to accept the reality of a given situation because the depressed person knows that they need to do something and

a.	They don't want to do it or

b.	They don't know how to do it.

My Choice Theory Approach With Depression

Working with clients who have chosen to depress (or any other emotional problem) is a simple process that one can even do on their own without going to a therapist. Before I outline the therapeutic process, I feel the need to clarify some things that contribute to unhappiness. There are events that occur in life such as tornados, hurricanes, wild fires, earthquakes, tsunamis, floods, living in a war-torn zone, etc. These certainly can lead to choosing to depress and they are events that commonly occur all over the world. But those who experience their depression as a result of those conditions are not the typical client that seeks help from counselors and therapists.

The clients I see are individuals who choose to depress (or other behaviors) because they are not experiencing the relationship that they would like to have with someone important to them. The reasons may be divorce, infidelity, death of a loved one, loss of employment, loss of health, or the behavior of someone else who is behaving in a disapproving manner. This disapproving behavior may even be that of the client him/herself. Examples of self-disapproving behaviors are gambling, alcohol and drug addiction, eating disorders, sex addiction, over-spending, emotional and other problems that cause social and relationship problems.

First: Indentify the problem.
Who in your life is behaving in a way in which you disapprove and how do you want things to be different?

Second: What have you been doing to make those things happen?

Third: How effective have your efforts been to make them happen?

Fourth: What can you do differently that you haven't done to get the results you wish?

Identify: Whatever a client may tell me is their reason to seek counseling, I already have it in my mind that it will be a problem rooted in an unsatisfactory relationship. What I find particularly interesting is the number of clients who deny they have a problem with someone else. This is usually due to not wanting to face the reality of the situation or else it may be of a personal concern that the client doesn't wish to disclose.

Unlike many other therapy procedures, I don't bother with probing into a client's past. Whatever the problem may be, it will always be something that is going on now, in the present. The problem may have started long ago but the situation is happening now. While the past may uncover the causes a client's behavior, it will have no benefit in dealing with the client's needs today. The past is something that cannot be changed no matter how hard one may try. Whatever happened, happened. Let's look at what we can do today to create happiness and maintain it in our tomorrows.

 After asking a client to give me a brief synopsis of what is going on in their life, I then cut right to the chase. If they haven't already disclosed conflict with another person and they report their problem is depression, anxiety, fear, anger, etc. I ask, "Who in your life are you having difficulty?" It will usually be a parent, a spouse or significant other, sibling, employer, friend, or perhaps even a teacher . . . people who are important to them. It won't be the paper delivery person who forgot to deliver a paper or the dry cleaners that said your suit would be ready by Wednesday, and it isn't.

Think about the time when you were, or are, unhappy. Most likely, it was because of an important person in your life who was behaving in a way that you find disapproving. It may even have been you.

Also, identify how you want the situation to resolve? What do you want to accomplish or get out of any resolution? Keep in mind, that the only person you can control is yourself so wanting another person to change is not a viable response.

 I once had a client, who I will call Josh, who was severely depressed. I recognized the look and body language right away from my own experiences. His face was pale, drawn, and the appearance of total despair. I asked him what his story was that was contributing to his sadness and he told me that his wife had left him . . . that he had come home from work and she and all her belongings were gone.

I then asked, "Why do you think she left you?"

He answered, "For the life of me, I really don't know." I replied, "I don't mean to be rude but it's been my experience that people don't leave someone because they are happy with them. They leave because they are unhappy. So what is it that you think you may have been doing that she found unacceptable? Don't tell me you don't know because I'm fairly sure she has told you several times what she dislikes about your behavior. If she were here, right now, what would she tell me that you do that she doesn't like? What is it that you have been doing that she complained and criticized you for doing?"

He thought for a moment and said, "I guess it would have to be that she thinks I don't give her credit to make her own decisions and that I *Parent* her." I asked, "What does that mean?" He said, "Well I know a lot of things about life that she doesn't so I'm teaching her." "So you "*teach*" her?" I asked. He said, "Yeah, it's for her own good." I replied, "Ah. I see. Does she ever "Parent" you?" He said, "No, but there's not much she could teach me anyway. She says I treat her like a child." I asked, "Would you like to be treated like a child?" He said, "No, of course not." I said, "Neither did she and that's why she left. I think she just taught you something."

I asked him what he wanted to gain from seeing me today. He said, "I want you to get her back for me." I informed him that we counselors don't have that kind of power to control others and get them to do something that they may not want to do. I told him I could help him with his unhappiness but that he would have to be the person to take any measures to get her back and then . . . there would be no guarantee that she would return.

What have you done so far?

I asked him what he had done, so far, to get her back. He told me "nothing." I asked, "Did you try to call her?" He told me he had no idea where she was. I asked, "If you *did* know where she was, where do you think that would be?" He said, "I don't know." I said, "So if you haven't done anything and you haven't tried to locate her. How well do you think those methods might help you two get back together? Do you think she will just come back home on her own, forgive you, and all will be okay if she does?"

I said, "I don't even know your wife but I'm sure I could find her if I had to. Does she have a mother?" He said, "Of course she does." I said, "What are the odds that her mother would know where she is?"

A person can choose to be so depressed that they may not be able to think clearly and logically. It is at these times that some people may make other poor choices that make their situation much worse than it is or even keep them from being creative enough to find their own answers to their problems.

I could tell he was choosing to get a bit upset with me. Actually, he was getting upset with himself and transferring his anger onto me. He said, "You don't take this very seriously, do you?" I said, "I find it very serious. A wife doesn't pack up all she owns and leave her home and husband because she's happy. But you're the one she left so I choose not to feel all the unhappiness you are feeling. I have empathy for your situation but I don't care to feel as badly as you choose to feel."

He got even more indignant. "You keep saying "choose" to feel. Do you think I'm *choosing* to feel this miserable? I'd have to be out of my right mind to do something like that." I said, "If you look around my office, you will notice all these credentials and licenses I have on my wall. This is a counselor's office. No one in their right mind comes to see me." He couldn't hold back and he let out a laugh.

"Tell me . . . were you just now feeling sad when you felt a little annoyed? Did you feel sad just now when you laughed?" He admitted he didn't. "That means you chose to react based upon whatever you were thinking at the time you changed from sad, to angry, to laughter. You thought I was not taking your seriously and you chose to get a bit upset. You could have just let it go but you didn't. You could have remained sad when I told you about the "out of your mind" thing and you could have chosen to continue to be angry or return to sadness. The fact is, you can't be depressing and angry and happy at the same time. You could have easily stayed with one emotion . . . sadness, anger, or laughing. You chose to do all of them within a span of three minutes based upon whatever you were perceiving at the time. All of our emotions are the result of whatever we are thinking.

"Do you feel physically good when you are sad?" He answered, "No, of course not. I feel weak, tired, achy, and even nauseous." I asked, "Did you feel physically good when you began to get annoyed with me?" He said, "No. I was beginning to feel angry, tense, and stressed." I then asked, "So how did you feel just now when you laughed?" He said, "I felt good. I felt a bit relieved and happy for a bit."

So here's my point: If you are sad or angry, or any other unhappy emotion, it will be because of whatever you are thinking at the time. When you felt happy it's because of what you were thinking and what you were doing . . . laughing. Whichever emotion you were choosing at the time had an effect on how you felt physically . . . all based upon what you were thinking and doing. So the key to controlling how we feel from being sad to happy is to change what we are thinking and/or change what we are doing . . . our behavior.

I didn't want to get into an involved Choice Theory training session with Josh at this time. He was not in a good state of mind to learn the intricacies of Choice Theory right then. I asked him if his wife had a close friend or a mother and he said she did. I suggested he call one or the other to inquire about the whereabouts of his wife so that he might be able to attempt to resolve their conflict. To make a long story of several counseling sessions short, he did make contact and his wife and she was not willing to work out their difficulty. She soon filed for divorce.

I continued to see Josh and show him how to apply Choice Theory to his life. He took to it quickly and reported that it had not only helped him in his personal life but in his business life in sales dealing with customers. He soon met someone else and he wanted her to learn Choice Theory too. I saw them both prior to their marriage and how to resolve any future conflict with Choice Theory concepts. So far, this marriage has lasted more than his previous marriage and he calls from time to time to report life is going well for them both. He admits they each have their moments but now they know how to resolve them.

No one can be happy all the time. Life and things can often occur that results in unhappiness. These things are often unavoidable. Knowing and applying Choice Theory is the most effective means that I have found to help others find happiness.

To recap, Josh identified the problem. He then saw that what he had been doing wasn't working not only for the marriage but no plan to get back in touch with her even though he wanted to. He then planned to call someone who would know of her whereabouts, (her mother) and made contact. They eventually met, got back together long enough to see me and it was then that his wife had already decided she no longer wanted to be married to Josh so that was the finality of their marriage.

Josh reacted to the failed marriage better than his initial discovery that his wife had left him by using the concepts of Choice Theory. By now, he was ready to accept the reality of the situation and deal with it by choosing how he would react to the results. During the six months they were separated, Josh had found someone else, which is usually the case for young couples after a breakup or divorce. Newfound love and acceptance played a part in helping him accept and get over his failed marriage. He had replaced the image of his wife in his Quality World with an image of his new girlfriend. Both he and his new bride learned Choice Theory and their marriage is holding strong for the last several years to date.

> *It is almost impossible for anyone, even the most ineffective among us, to continue to choose misery after becoming aware that it is a choice.*
>
> *- William Glasser*

Karen

It is not uncommon for some of my clients to deny that they are having difficulty with another person in their life and that the current situation with them is the actual cause of their unhappiness. I am still amazed when this happens. Perhaps it is because they don't want to have to admit to the reality of the problem or that they simply don't want to discuss it. The following is just one example of many such cases I have encountered:

Karen is a person I was introduced to by way of a mutual acquaintance. When she discovered that I was a counselor, she disclosed that she had been prescribed Prozac and was currently taking it and not liking how it made her feel.

Karen was not a client but when someone talks to me about behavior and psychiatric drugs, I automatically turn into Counselor Man sans the cape. I asked her how long she had been taking the drug. She reported she had been taking it for the last four months. You probably know by now what my next question to her was. I asked, "What was going on in your life some four months ago? Where you experiencing an unsatisfying relationship with someone important to you? Karen almost instantly replied, "No, not at all."

So then I reworded the question: "Is someone in your life not behaving the way you would like them to?"

Again, she replied, "No." So I dropped the questions and shared my short-version opinion about psychiatric drugs while slyly interjecting that people choose to feel bad for a reason and that it just doesn't happen out of the blue.

I then tried to change the subject because I didn't want to play "counselor" anymore, especially with someone who wasn't a client in the first place. But Karen wasn't about to let my statement go about people "choosing" to feel depressed. She became a bit angry and said, "You mean I'm taking this damn medication for nothing?" Now I felt boxed in. I felt like Lucile Ball did when Ricky Arnez would say to her, "You've got some 'splainin' to do."

I didn't want to get into a full discussion about Depression or her situation. I was in a social gathering with others at the time and I already had spent too much time in the office that day. I explained that there is no chemical imbalance of serotonin as it was commonly being told to the public about depression and that their sadness was the direct result of having an unsatisfying relationship with the important people in their lives. I then advised her not to stop taking her meds just because of what I had said but that if she wanted to do so, she would need to seek the medical supervision of her doctor first. So then I changed the subject and we talked about other things.

Several months went by and the friend that had introduced Karen to me disclosed information that was behind all of Karen's depression. Karen had undergone open-heart surgery about a year before I met her. It turns out that there were two important people in her life afterwards who were not behaving the way she preferred: Herself with her poor heart condition, and her husband, who no longer appeared to want any sexual relations with her after the surgery.

Surgery, alone, would not be an unusual cause of depressing. It's not easy for any of us to have to face dire health conditions and our mortality. Postoperative surgery depressing is very common. The person who is not behaving the way they would like them to behave is their self.

It was at this time that she began to perceive her husband's apparent lack of sexual interest in her to be the result of her aging and loss of sexual appeal.

Not wanting to admit to her mortality and sexual problem to a complete stranger, like myself, is why she denied having any difficulty with anyone in her life. As it turned out, her husband was caring for her health more than satisfying his sexual urges. He didn't want to cause or be part of any undue stress she might incur after having heart surgery. As time went by and she recovered from her heart condition, their sexual life returned to what it had been in the past. And for all of this, she was prescribed mental illness medication.

While Karen was not a client of mine, many clients I see do avoid disclosing any unsatisfying relationship going on in their life, at first. Simply allowing the client to talk will eventually uncover any relationship conflicts. On the other hand, I have far more clients who are more than willing to tell me all about someone they are having problems with. Some of their stories seem endless and I find myself telling them that I get the picture and that there's no need for them to go on and on about how unhappy they are.

You can't finish a book if you keep reading the same chapter over and over.

Chapter 10 - Why The Past Is Not Worth Delving Into

When I was in school learning to be a counselor, we were automatically trained that a person's "mental illness," or "issues," were the direct result of something that happened to them in the past or during their development. The goal of the counselor was then to explore the client's past and try to discover or unearth what traumatic event occurred in the past, or what they may have failed to receive in development that is the cause of their misery and perhaps unconventional or unwanted behavior.

I'm reminded of the saying, "Whatever doesn't kill you makes you stronger." Many times, however, whatever doesn't kill you may also lead to creating unhealthy and maladaptive behaviors that often creates other problems in your life.

Digging into a client's past became my specialty very early in my career. I would ask many questions and probe for anything that would indicate a change in the client's behavior. I looked for such things as the client avoiding the question or anything about a particular person in their life; a change in tone and volume of their voice; saddened expressions, squirming in their chair, etc, etc. My goal was to "hit the client's buttons" that would cause an obvious reaction of emotion, expression, body language. Once I found a reaction to something I would say to myself, "BINGO! I found it!" and pat myself on the back for being so good at what I do.

Then the clients, who were functioning in a fairly normal way when they came to me, would now begin to feel miserable the more I got them to talk about their past. Some would refuse to talk about it at all in which case I would inform them that the only way for them to overcome their problem in life was to "work through" whatever happened to them in the past. They would then leave my office feeling worse than they did when they first walked in. Some would not even come back for a second session. I wonder why?

I was conducting my counseling techniques just as I had been trained to do so I didn't see anything wrong with what I had been doing. In fact, I considered myself to be very good at discovering clients' reasons for their behavior dependent upon that method. After several months, I began to self-evaluate the success of my counseling. While there were some who found their own way out of their unhappiness, I became aware that the majority of them were no better off than they had been when they first came to see me. What bothered me the most was that much of the time, clients would leave my office feeling worse than they did when they first walked in. What I was doing suddenly didn't feel right. I didn't see any real success to my technique or perceive this as being helpful or to any advantage for the client. "Good grief!   What if one of them felt so badly after meeting with me that they committed suicide?"

After discovering Dr. Glasser's book, "Choice Theory," I began to feel validated in my own thoughts about the ineffectiveness or, at best . . . the slowing down of my therapeutic process with clients. Now I was beginning to understand why Reality Therapy did not rely on dealing with a client's past.

> *Glasser would say*, *"What happened in the past that was painful has a great deal to do with what we are today, but revisiting this painful past can contribute little or nothing to what we need to do now."*

I began to only discuss what is happening today, right now, with my clients and asking them what it is that they hoped to get out of seeing me. This made a noticeable change in the demeanor of my clients as well as the effectiveness of my counseling.

Some clients who had received previous counseling with other therapists would ask, "Aren't you going to ask me about my past?" It's almost as if they can't wait to tell me some sordid story about their past. Some had previously been labeled with a mental illness diagnosis and because an "expert" said they had a specific diagnosis . . . they wore it like a badge of honor. Those who did that seemed to do so because it gave them an excuse for not taking responsibility for their own happiness.

I often hear from clients, "I have PTSD" or "I have Schizophrenia," or "I'm ADD," and "I'm Bipolar." You can have diabetes, cancer, pancreatitis, COPD, heart disease, and other medical conditions but you can't *have* anything that doesn't have any physical pathology. The DSM correctly identifies the behaviors of what they have incorrectly labeled "diseases." What they have are the behaviors of labeled disorders. They are *acting* or *displaying* the behaviors of unhappiness.

Those who wish to disclose their unhappy past with me will do so even when I tell them that it's not important at this time. I sometimes ask, "Does talking about your unhappy past make you happy?" When they say, "No, it does just the opposite." Then I reply, "So why do you want to go there? Whatever happened to you in the past is something that had a drastic effect on you mentally, emotionally, and perhaps even physically. Whatever that was, I'm very sorry that you experienced it. I mean that sincerely. But whatever it is that happened, did indeed happen and nothing you or I will ever say or do will ever change the fact that it happened. So why don't we talk about what you would like to have in your life that you feel is missing? Since we can't change the past, how can we change today and tomorrow to make them better days?

Some of the people I have counseled have wanted to go back and relive the past even at the cost of emotional pain. When I ask them, "Why do you want to dwell on something that happened that you can't change?" The most common response I get is, "because I want to know WHY it happened." I ask, "If you knew why would your life get any better? You may know why your tooth aches but it will still ache until you go to your dentist. Concentrating on your tooth won't make the pain go away. It will only make it worse."

This procedure gets directly to the wants and desires of the client; helps them to put the past behind them, and discover new ways to get their needs met. I have associates who rely on focusing on the past with their clients. I ask them, "Why do you do that?" They tell me, "To get to the core issues of the client's problems." Then I ask them how long it takes for them to discover the problems from their client's past. They tell me it sometimes takes several sessions before the client trusts them enough to tell them about their past and that can sometimes take several weeks.

Then I ask them what do they do after they have discovered their client's past "core issues." They tell me that they discuss the events that happened and figure out why they were abused emotionally or physically by someone else and how they feel about it. Then they discuss how to deal with whatever happened to them. I ask, "How long does that take?" They tell me that the process will take anywhere from a few months to a couple of years depending upon the severity of their past experience. Not only do my associates and other professionals believe this to be a successful form of treatment, it also insures them a steady income.

Then I ask, "What is the desired outcome that the client wants to receive by coming to see you?" They tell me that ultimately their clients want to put the past behind them, find happiness, and get on with their life. So then I ask, "Then why not start there on your first meeting with them instead of spending all that time helping them to feel bad, helpless, perhaps blaming others for their unhappiness, and obsessing over something that cannot be changed. It also prohibits them taking responsibility for their own happiness, as well as costing them a lot of money? Some of my associates look at me like I'm naive. Others have no response because they don't see it that way and don't know what to say other than shrug their shoulders as if to say, "I don't know". A few will smile and say, "Hey, I gotta pay the rent."

Personally, I want my clients to leave feeling better after each session than they did when they first walked into my office . . . even if it's just for little bit. I don't care to waste the client's or my time by dealing with things and people that can't be changed and that slows the counseling process down or even impede its success. I've gone that route. It is not nearly as effective as when using Reality Therapy and Choice Theory.

The pain suffered in the past has had an effect on one's motivation . . . either in a positive way to rise above it or negatively . . .to remain stuck in a victim role with unhealthy survival techniques. We have eyes in the front of our face to look forward and not backwards.

I have never had a client make an appointment because they were having difficulty dealing with their happiness. Every client I have ever seen came to me because they were unhappy. I know this to be true before they even walk into my office. So what should the mutual goal for my clients and me be? For them to discover how to be happy and get their happiness needs met.

Chapter 11 - Alcohol and Drugs

Another very common way people ease their unhappiness is with alcohol and illicit drugs. These drugs simply numb the brain and keep it from functioning the way it is supposed to function. The other method is by way of pharmaceutical drugs. Psychotropic medications numb the brain also and stop the brain's ability to be creative. This is why these medications have no curative abilities.

Psych meds only cause the brain to stop functioning normally and shut down their brain's ability to solve or work out their own unhappiness in more healthy ways. This is why those taking these medications for years are often told they have to take them for the rest of their life.

Before taking the medication, a person may have created some type of behavior, such as depression, anxiety, phobias, obsessive/compulsive, or any other behavior that may be considered a mental illness. These are behaviors that they created to deal with and ease their unhappiness. You may not be able to see how their behavior is working for them but it does to an extent. At least it eases their unhappiness to a more tolerable state of being. Their chosen behaviors may not totally satisfy their unmet needs but they are their best attempt at the time that provides them with some form of satisfaction.

For those who do not work in the field of addictions (and for some who do), there have been numerous articles attributed to the "Cause of Addiction." The authors of these articles start out with the best of intentions believing that they have discovered the cause of addiction. It seems as quickly as they begin with their findings, a switch seems to go off sending them onto a totally different track resulting in information that has always been known: Alcohol and drugs are addictive and people who drink and use do so "to feel better." Then the writers begin to describe all the reasons WHY people drink or use drugs without ever disclosing what causes the addiction.

They could have easily just written a short statement that said: "The cause of addiction is the result of drinking or using an addictive substance."

Not everyone who drinks or uses drugs become addicted to them. While it is true that you cannot become addicted to them unless you drink or use, the cause of the addiction is the consistent and constant use of the drug that is addictive over time. Anyone who drinks/uses long enough and hard enough will become addicted. So yes, what leads to addiction is the result of why people drink/use in the first place but those reasons are not the cause of addiction.

The cause of alcohol and drug addiction is bio-cellular. It is not a medical disease and it is not a mental illness. Many people believe it is a mental illness because of all of the "crazy" behavior an addict or alcoholic does when under the influence. Addiction is a non-infectious condition and no gene has yet to be confirmed to identify it as a genetic condition (although many have claimed or believe it to be without solid proof or confirmation).

Once a person crosses the lines of sociological and psychological reasons for their usage, they eventually cross the biochemical line and become physiologically addicted. Over time, millions of cells become altered to deal with the regular presence of the substance. These cells adjust from the way they were naturally meant to function and are now functioning differently with the substance that is regularly being used. After any period of depravation, these cells react in what might be called violent ways. The cells no longer are getting the drug they have been accustomed to getting and this leads to several different physical reactions (withdrawal) that also lead to emotional reactions..

A true physically addict or alcoholic feels "sick" when not getting their drugs or alcohol. They drink or use to "feel well." I refer to a "true" addict/alcoholic as one who has crossed that biochemical line. All others are primarily drug/alcohol abusers and not addicted . . . yet. . . . at least not biochemically.

NOW you can talk about why people drink or use drugs. To seek the pleasant for the unpleasant is the most natural thing we do as humans. . If cold, we put on a coat or sweater. If it rains, we go inside or seek other shelter. If hot, we turn on the AC. If we have a headache, we take an aspirin. If stressed or anxious, some rely on drugs or alcohol. When relationships go bad, crawling into a bottle or drug use is a temporary fix to numb unwanted and uncomfortable emotions. If an addict or alcoholic feels "sick" s/he drinks or uses to feel better. This is why so many individuals relapse or even fail to begin treatment. They are avoiding the symptoms of withdrawal (which can be extremely severe).

Not everyone who abuses alcohol or drugs for the above-mentioned reasons become biochemically addicted. Those who have resolved their "unpleasant" issues before ever crossing the biochemical line eventually *may* become normal drinkers or no longer rely on drugs. However, I don't usually tell my clients this bit of information.

The person who has, unfortunately, crossed that biochemical line <u>cannot</u> return to normal drinking or using.

Overcoming addiction is much more of a challenge than merely ceasing one's habitual behavior. They have to overcome two very difficult psychological reasons for drinking and using and then one bio-chemical cause of their addiction.

After having gone through withdrawals and detoxification, and regardless of the years they may be abstinent, cells retain a memory of how to function with the presence of drugs/alcohol. Should the drugs be reintroduced, the addictive process re-awakens relatively quickly. In a short time, the addict/alcoholic finds him/herself worse off than they were before they quit. This is why a true, bio-chemical alcoholic/addict cannot return to responsible use.

So what is the cause of addiction? It isn't unhappiness, stress, loneliness, etc. Those are the reasons *why* people drink or use drugs. The cause of addiction is cellular mutation caused by consistent usage forcing cells to change and adjust with the presence of the drug of choice. These cells now rely on the substance in order to function under their newly acquired modification. During any period of deprivation, these cells react violently causing several physical reactions that can even result in death. Not wanting to have these reactions and wanting to feel better is why they continue to drink or use as well as relapsing after having stopped for any period of time.

In Choice Theory, emphasis is placed on thinking and/or behaving to resolve unhappiness. Emotional and physiological aspects are affected indirectly based on thinking and behaving. In the addict's world, drugs and alcohol have a direct and instantaneous effect on emotions and physiological conditions without any concern for thinking and behaving . . . other than choosing to use/drink to feel better. They have learned that drugs and alcohol are the most efficient tools in their behavioral system for effective, albeit temporary, relief of their unwanted emotions and physical illness symptoms. Ironically, the substance that causes their unwanted conditions is what is relied upon to alleviate them.

Shopaholics, sexaholics, and gambling addicts don't have biochemical addictions but they do have an addiction to pleasure, which they misinterpret as happiness. Since the pleasure is short-lived, the behavior must be repeated often to maintain the feeling of pleasure. If they cease their behaviors, they will experience emotional withdrawals but not necessarily physical withdrawals other than those that may be created by their emotional being. Dr. Wm. Glasser reminds us that pleasure is easily attained without the involvement of other people and happiness can only be attained by maintaining meaningful relationships. The late noted psychiatrist, Victor Frankl, tells us, those who have found no meaning to their lives find it easy to resort to things that bring pleasure.

I'm often asked, "If we choose all that we do, then why do people choose to be alcoholics?" Those wishing to challenge the concept that we choose our behaviors ask me this question often. Is alcoholism a choice? Before I respond to that question, we need to look at why people drink alcohol in the first place.

Over the last twenty-five years, eighty per cent of my clients have been substance abusers or compulsive drinkers/users. I've had a passing fancy with it myself. You can say it is my specialty as I have worked with over four thousand alcohol and drug abusers and addicts over the years.

The average person has their first drink of alcohol around the age of fifteen. The first time you had an alcoholic drink, you might recall that it did not taste good at all. What it did do, however, was create a feeling of euphoria. It could be said that your first drink was a sensation more than it was a taste.

From the sensation came the desire to experience the sensation again, regardless of the taste. In simple terms, you liked the way it made you feel. If it didn't do that, you couldn't give it away. The more the sensation was desired, the more one is able to acquire a taste for it. In other words . . . become accustomed to the taste for the sake of the sensation. You liked how you felt indifferent about what others might think of you or what image you feel you have to project to others. Your inhibitions lowered so much that you began to feel relaxed, worry-free, and perhaps some feelings of elation.

Current emotions would become exaggerated. You felt pleasure, which you confused for happiness. You were in the midst of others who were experiencing the same things along with you. Everyone saw each other as pleasing, fun, and acceptable. You probably laughed more and talked more. If an introvert, you became an extrovert. If worried, you felt apathetic toward whatever was bothering you. If weak you became fearless. You came out and said things that you would normally keep bottled up inside and now was easing all of your tension and stress. You had found a magic elixir that released you from all of those things that were consuming your unpleasant thoughts and unhappiness.

Not everyone who consumes alcohol has this awareness, acquires a taste, or has a fondness for the potion. There are those who feel they don't like to lose control of their thoughts and behaviors. If they drink at all, it would be sparingly and in social situations only. They may even opt for some other beverage rather than alcohol. The same applies for those who use drugs. There are also those who may have a glass of wine occasionally when dining out. They generally won't have more than one or 2 glasses of wine and then have no more. There are also those who may wish to have a drink when they come home from work . . . to "relax" or "unwind." Again . . . they are drinking for the effect more than for the taste and this, alone, is not necessarily an addicted person. So why do people drink? They drink for the effect. They like how it makes them feel. If it didn't do that, they would never drink or use.

Is there anyone who has not heard or is not aware of the fact that alcohol or some dugs are addictive substances? If you are aware that what you are consuming is addictive and yet you continue to consume it regardless . . . is that not a choice?

In Choice Theory, we know that the four components of Total Behavior are Thinking, Feeling, Physiology, and Acting. Of those four components, we have direct control of only two of them: Thinking and Acting. But there is always an exception to the rule. There are two things that DO have a direct effect on one's emotions and physiology: Alcohol and drugs, including prescription drugs. There are very few prescription drugs that cure any of the major so-called mental illnesses from which people have been diagnosed. A great many of our prescription drugs, at best, only mask symptoms by drugging the brain or keep the condition in check without a cure. Illegal drugs and alcohol can do much of the same thing and one doesn't generally have to wait very long for them to take effect and are easily attained without a prescription.

I don't know of anyone who has said, "I think I'll become addicted to alcohol (or meth, cocaine, heroin, cannabis, etc). All addicts/alcoholics have several things in common. One of those commonalities is how they became addicts/alcoholics in the first place. They discovered that they got pleasure from drinking and using as well as it being a cure, albeit temporary, for those things that are pressing on their mind.

They are actually anesthetizing their brain and numbing all of their unwanted emotions.

To seek to satisfy the unpleasant with something pleasant is a natural human behavior. The actions we take to satisfy these unpleasant situations are all choices. Alcohol and drugs provide relief for other displeasures such as conflict with spouses, relationships, jobs, kids, debt, grief, anger, disappointments, tension, anxiety, and sadness. They also contribute to the loss of spouse, family, friends, jobs, income, health, and death.

While being fully aware that drugs and alcohol are addictive substances, the false belief that one is in control of his/her use is why they become addicted. They believe they will be able to recognize if and when their use becomes a problem. Others will always recognize the addiction long before the alcoholic or addict ever sees it.   Once the cellular structure of one's brain, organs, and muscles, have been altered due to regular and continued use, the body can no longer function without the substance without going through physical and emotional discomfort. This condition is more commonly recognized as withdrawal symptoms.

Withdrawal symptoms can be very severe and are always unpleasant. They can even lead to death. After any period of deprivation, when the cells do not receive their alcohol/drugs, they sort of revolt and readjust causing some physical complications and emotional distress. So if we can control our temperature discomfort, our hunger/thirst discomfort, and our need for shelter, we can also control our withdrawal symptoms by giving the cells that which they are accustomed that will end the suffering . . . more drugs and alcohol. Ironically, the substance that is causing all of the suffering is what is being relied upon to end the suffering.

The most insidious aspect of addition is that the addict/alcoholic is totally unaware that they are addicted even when everyone else around them can see it. This phenomenon is known in the psychiatric world as "anosognosia." Both the physical body and the socio-psychological part of the brain have become dependent on the substance. When an unhappy person is faced with the reality that they don't have the things they want in life that provide them with happiness, the realization that they are out of control and addicted will only add fuel to their unhappiness. When all their present known abilities to satisfy their unhappiness have failed, they have learned that drugs and alcohol will always make them feel better, if only on a temporary basis. Therefore, they have to continue to drink or use in order to feel better. By not drinking or using, they would feel much worse and unhappy. They know no other way to ease their frustration. It would be too painful, emotionally and physically, for them to stop drinking or using.

So is their addiction a choice? Yes. However it is an indirect choice. One first becomes reliant on drinking/using to satisfy social needs and interacting with others is a spirit of happiness, socializing, and comradery . . . a social addiction. About the same time, one learns that drugs/alcohol is a quick fix to overcome unwanted emotions from unwanted situations. This awareness leads to a psychological component of addiction. The perception of their use at this time is not one of being addicted. They perceive it as a way of acquiring relief from any unhappiness they may be experiencing.

The next stage is when one crosses over the line into cellular adaptation. This is the result of regular or consistent use of the substance. Some may take a long period of time before this happens while others may become addicted relatively quickly. The cellular structure of the body eventually changes its structure to function with the continued presence of the substance. The addict/alcoholic gets blindsided and doesn't see it coming. They are now physically addicted yet still refuse to believe it.

The overall dependency is now so strong that they refuse to believe they are out of control. They believe that they actually need it in order to survive and feel "normal." And when they eventually do realize they are addicted, they are still defiant against sobriety because they don't possess the means to deal with their unhappiness without it. They have tried everything else that they know in order to find happiness so they are not aware of anything else they can do besides rely on their drug of choice. They know they can rely on their drugs or alcohol and it has practically instant results. They feel physically ill if not drinking or using and feel better when they use. Nothing else will work as quickly than their using or drinking in order to feel better.

If given a choice between instant gratification versus five days of detoxification and ninety or more days of rehab and months or years of learning new ways to deal with life on life's terms . . . which one do you think an addict or alcoholic will choose?

If someone has to put something into their body in order to feel happy, they are missing some of their genetic needs for happiness and are only temporarily masking their unhappiness. They are seeking control of their life with a substance that causes loss of control. They have not learned how to find happiness by breathing pure air and have found no better way, at the time, to acquire what they consider to be happiness even though they feel miserable. There is no happiness pill. There are only brain and emotional numbing drugs to mask unhappiness. At best, drugs and alcohol can only provide pleasure and not happiness.

The addict and alcoholic leave a trail of wreckage behind them in their addiction. Not only do they trip over the messes they make, but they bring with them all those who love and live with them.

Addiction is called an insidious behavior and truly it is. Of all the damage it causes to the addict and their loved ones, one of the most damaging effects begin with the onset of the addiction. From the moment they begin to abuse drugs and alcohol, they stop the learning process and creative skills needed to be learned the entire time of their abuse and addiction. If and whenever they stop drinking and or using, life doesn't just automatically become "normal." They have failed to learn and develop the healthy coping skills that life with now throw at them in their clean and sober life.

As difficult as it is to stop drinking and using . . . and believe me . . . stopping the use is extremely difficult . . . it is still the easiest part of overcoming addiction. The hard part is learning all of the things they failed to learn when they were drinking and using. Abstinence is one thing. Recovery is another. Recovery is where one must learn the things they failed to receive when drinking and using. This is where Alcoholics Anonymous comes into play. The Twelve-Steps of A.A., along with a sponsor, consists of the steps needed to acquire the necessary life skills that were never learned.

Kevin and Andrea

Kevin came to me as a requirement from the legal system in an upper Midwestern state to be assessed for anger management and domestic violence. After completing several questionnaires regarding his history of anger and violence, it was apparent that his temperament was not out of the ordinary of most other people. Yes, he had his moments of emotional conflict over his 38 years but mostly those that caused harm to himself more than someone else. Kevin shared his story with me as to how he ended up in this situation in the first place. He stated that his girlfriend, Andrea, is addicted to alcohol and that she often makes things up as a means to control others and get attention as well as to divert anyone who attempts to get her to stop drinking. Kevin is trying to control something that he has no power to control: getting back together. He can only do whatever he can for himself.

Kevin stated that he did, indeed, lose his temper but that he never laid a hand on Andrea. He stated that he got angry when she became intoxicated after having been sober for 3 months and that he threw a framed photograph that broke and left shattered glass all over the floor. He stated that she tried to avoid the glass and fell against a coffee table causing a red mark on her left arm. Kevin explained that he gets so upset with Andrea when she has been drinking that he does lose his temper but only raised his voice to her with no physical contact or threats. Being a tall man of six foot two looming over a five foot three inch person can be very intimidating to someone who is intoxicated at the time.

Kevin stated that someone in the apartment complex called the police after hearing the disturbance and that Andrea told them that Kevin had grabbed her and threw her down after throwing the photograph. Kevin was arrested for disorderly conduct as well as domestic violence. Andrea saw a therapist who diagnosed her as schizophrenic and gave her a prescription for a highly potent psych med, which should never be taken with alcohol. The therapist was diagnosing a drug-affected person's behavior with no concern for her addiction to alcohol. Many a misdiagnosis is made in this manner.

Andrea continued to drink while taking her medication, which has several possible dangerous side effects of their own that are increased when used with alcohol. Her behavior became more erratic and Kevin continued to "save" her from her demons and alcohol addiction. He reports that both of them left the Midwest and moved to Arizona to start a new life. This is a common practice of alcoholics called geographic relocation with the intent of starting over and getting away from all the wreckage they caused themselves and others. While they left their hometown, Kevin could not escape his legal obligation to his home state. He was required to receive counseling for his anger and domestic violence issues.

After interviewing Kevin, I became more concerned for his addiction to Andrea than his anger issues (although one often leads to the other). He was giving up his own wants and needs for the sake of Andrea's wants and needs by trying to help her beat her addiction. As a result, she is consuming all of his thoughts and he is fighting a losing battle to get her sober while not tending to his own responsibilities and needs.

I recommended he complete an anger management program in order to satisfy the court back in the Midwest. What he really needs is to start focusing on his own needs, which do not include Andrea's alcohol use. He is making her problem his problem and consuming most of his day-to-day thoughts. I told him in no uncertain terms that he cannot and never will get Andrea to stop drinking and that both of them need professional help for their problems: She to an inpatient program and he to Al-anon and get co-dependency counseling. What they both need is to get away from each other and walk away and learn ways to deal with controlling their own individual lives in a more effective manner and then getting back together.

The primary concern for Andria would be to get into an inpatient or intensive outpatient treatment program for addiction and become involved in Alcoholics Anonymous with the acquisition of a sponsor who will take her through each of the twelve steps of A.A. Then she would do well to focus on taking responsibility for her own happiness and dealing with life's adversities without facing or avoiding them with alcohol. She could create some new and more effective survival skills and improve her relationships with those whom she has harmed due to her addiction as well as improve her relationship with herself. In fact, all of Andrea's basic needs are in need of self-evaluation and improvement in order for her to acquire the happiness and life she would really like to have.

Kevin has strong love and belonging needs but his attempts to get these needs met have all been backfiring on him. The more needy a person is for love, the more they are inclined to make the wrong choices . . . not only in choosing a partner but also their methods to help others. He has become enmeshed in her life to the point where you can't tell where one of them ends and the other person begins. While Kevin took note of my informing him that he will not ever be successful in getting Andrea to stop drinking, unless he addresses his own neediness for love, he will be in for the rollercoaster ride of his life and they will both be caught up in the muck and mire of addiction. Without help, their lives will get much worse before they ever get better.

Moving from the Midwest to Arizona will only change the scene but not the roles each of them have been playing. What has been going on in the Midwest will only continue to play out in a different location. The more Kevin tries to save Andrea from her addiction, the more frustrated and angry he will get. The more Kevin tries to save Andrea from her addiction, the more angry she will become and will eventually leave him for someone else who doesn't try to change her. There will be more arguments and calls to the police with her claiming domestic violence and abuse and neighbors claiming peace disturbance. In some cases, situations like this can and do play out with even worse scenarios with physical abuse and even death.

Anger

Anger is a natural emotion. I say that because many a new-born child often comes into this world letting their feelings be known under no uncertain terms. Many an infant emerges practically screaming. They have been comfortably situated in their mother's womb for several months and now they are in a cold environment with bright lights and unfamiliar sounds, and being grabbed and tugged with things being stuck up their nose. They aren't happy.

As we become older, there are several things that can occur that can lead to choosing to react in anger. In almost every case, the situation will involve someone else. Someone is behaving in a way in which you disapprove. It can also be a situation, or an object that isn't working, or your own failure to successfully fix something that is broken . . . including relationships. Anger can also appear when something wanted is expected or hoped for and it doesn't happen. One can also choose to become angry with themselves for their own perceived shortcomings. When things don't go the way we want them to, a common human reaction is to choose disappointment, anger, or depression.

I will be the first to tell you that I experience anger a couple of times each week. In my case, it always involves someone in traffic who does something that is illegal, is dangerous to others, themselves, or causes me to have to stop at traffic lights that I could have easily missed if the other driver hadn't done what they did. Driving slow in the fast lane when no one is in front of them is a pet peeve of mine.

Road range is seen all over the country. However, I never reach that stage of anger. In fact, my anger only lasts two to three seconds at most. But in that initial two or three seconds, I have been known to use language that would make a sailor blush. Fortunately, I never display or say what I say if someone else is in my car.

When I choose to anger, and after my seven syllable two word blast on their character ends, my Choice Theory knowledge kicks in and I chuckle each and every time it happens. I laugh at myself for reacting the way I chose to react at someone I don't even know and someone I most likely will never even meet. And since they are not someone who is important to me in my life, the anger is very short-lived. It ends almost as quickly as it takes to call them the names I chose to give them.

Then there are those who might experience the same traffic violators I do and choose to make it personal. They want revenge. They want the offender to know they have violated their space. How dare they do that to me! This is road rage and it puts everyone around them and themselves in danger. They do, indeed, have anger issues and have been harboring their anger for perhaps several years in their life. They perceive their life as being filled with people who have not been behaving the way they want them to behave. They perceive their world as threatening and full of disappointment and everyone not doing what they want them to do.

There are instances where a few police officers have had anger issues when they come across someone who is behaving in a way in which they disapprove. We have seen some videos of policemen who become violent with someone after a car or foot chase. Not all police officers behave in this manner. But those who do have this image in their Quality World of themselves as being powerful . . . power that they believe everyone should recognize because s/he wears a uniform, is armed, and "represents the law." To them, 'How dare you resist me! I'm the law! I have power over you!" They have been known to assault the offender and treat them roughly and get physical with them and even shoot them. Again, this is but a small percentage of our police officers. And when we see it, a natural anger arises that someone who is there to protect us and represents the law would behave in such a manner.

There are many police officers that behave in ways of respect and calmness with those who break laws but you don't see those videos on TV or social media. It seems that the American public wants to see those things that stirs their negative emotions and leads to their choosing to get upset and angry. It's as if their anger reminds them that they are alive because of the adrenalin rush, rise in blood pressure, stress and tenseness, and unhappiness that results from anger.

There are those who control their anger by choosing to depress. One cannot be angry and depressed at the same time. As Dr. Glasser reminds us, "Depression is a way to keep one's anger in check." Anger is the behavior one chooses to strike or lash outwardly. Depression is tuning anger inwardly that is commonly referred to as "stuffing one's anger." Outward expressions of anger are capable of harming others. Depression is capable of harming one's self.

The surest way to invoke anger is to utilize any of the seven distancing habits on another person. The receiver of such tactics then tends to use the same behaviors to the person who offended them. In either case, the behaviors of both are chosen behaviors to deal with each other.

Why can some people remain calm and unfazed when someone else does something offensive? One might say it's because of their character. While it may, indeed, be their character, it is their learned experience and knowledge of what to do that causes them the least amount of unhappiness. I'm reminded of two well-known entertainers Frank Sinatra and Dean Martin. Frank had a history of lasing out both verbally and physically when encountering someone who insulted him or behaved in disapproving behavior. Dean, on the other hand, always seemed to remain calm, make a joke, and casually let such matters dissolve. Once when Frank became unhappy with a patron at the Beverly Hills Polo Lounge, he hit the man. Dean looked at Frank, shook his head and said, "Why?" One's temperament is developed over time.

Some people are thin-skinned while others let things go like water off a duck's back. The control of one's anger issues can be learned by being aware that all our emotions are chosen based on our thoughts. The more one practices changing their thoughts to avoid feeling angry, the more they will get into the habit of catching themselves before it emerges.

One of my favorite sayings is, "if someone calls you a horse's ass, that's merely their opinion. But if three or more people call you a horse's ass, perhaps it's time to shop for a saddle."

It can't be said enough: When someone in your life is behaving in a way in which you disapprove, the first person who needs to change is yourself. You always have a choice on how to react to others in any given situation.

When a person is unhappy and their unhappiness or sadness turns to anger, a person will become frustrated in the fact that they have done all they know to do to make their unhappy and angry situation resolve. Their frustration only adds to their current angry state of mind and may lead them to choose drastic measures to end their unwanted and unhappy emotions. When feeling powerless about something, the tendency is to devise means and ways to create power, to feel in control, and to make their point to resolve their unhappiness. These are the individuals who recognize weapons to be the tool that will give them the power and ability to control others.

It appears that those who have yet to develop the skills to deal with their anger appropriately are those who rely on choices to use weapons or physical methods to deal with their unhappiness. Mostly, it is male between the ages of fifteen to twenty-five who resorts to mass shootings of people they don't even know. Since they are faceless and unknown beings to them, they find it easier to take their anger out on them.

In all of the school shootings, the offenders were under twenty-five and had relationship problems. They were either taking psychotropic drugs or had been taking them and some of these drugs are known to cause anger and even suicide. None of them were mentally ill but had been diagnosed as such to have been put on psych meds. They were, however, frustrated and angry . . . loners . . . detached from others with very little, if any, of their genetic needs for happiness being met. Their choice to shoot many unknown individuals was their way of feeling they had power and control . . . something they felt they didn't have until the time of their actions.

Psychiatric drugs can lead to violence. At best, these drugs only temporarily immobilize people from committing violence. It isn't until they stop taking them that they may resort to violence. Likewise, none of these drugs keep anyone from committing suicide but they can cause one to have suicidal thoughts and behavior. They even warn the patient that the drug may have this effect on them. Every school shooter had been taking psych meds at one time or another.

The military is aware of brain development in younger men and boys. There is a reason why young men drafted in wartime are between the ages of eighteen to twenty-five. When younger than twenty-five, there is a area in the frontal lobes of the brain that have yet to develop to the point of recognizing the full consequences of their behavior. A young man who feels he is invincible will take more risks than an older man. The older man will be much more reluctant to take risks that could easily be his ultimate demise. The most devastating life-threatening results are made by the young man between the ages of fifteen and twenty-five whose last words were, "Hey! Watch this!"

Domestic violence is nothing new. It has been around since the birth of mankind. It has become more of a public issue in the last thirty years. It is always the result of one person in the relationship not behaving the way the other person in the relationship want them to behave. When the seven habits of external control fail to be effective to control the other person, they resort to physical behavior. Again, the situation has come to the point of frustration where nothing else has worked to change the other person to get them to do what they want them to do so they lash out in anger and get physical. It can be wrestling, slapping, hitting, kicking, scratching, biting, pushing and shoving, and even the use of a knife or gun. Whatever the cause and whatever the choice of behavior to control . . . it is all done in anger and frustration.

Let's face it. We all experience anger from time to time. How many times did you ever choose anger when it didn't involve someone else? When did your anger ever get you the results you wanted? Worse yet . . . when did your anger ever make your unhappy situation worse or even result in physical harm to you or someone else?

Anger is a problem if it:

- o Occurs too often.
- o Lasts too long.
- o Is too intense.
- o Causes problems for self and others.

I recall a client in one of my group sessions who came to group with a bandaged hand that he had not had in previous group sessions. I asked, "What happened to your hand?" He replied, "I got angry with my girlfriend." So I asked facetiously, "What did she do? Bite your hand?" He answered, "No. I slammed my fist into the wall." I replied, "Boy, you sure showed her." Here is a case of one feeling so angry, frustrated, and out of control that he hit the wall and not her. He caused damage to his hand that required medical treatment and medical costs. Checking for his perception of the incident, I questioned him by asking, "So she made you hit the wall?" He was wise enough to say, "No. I was stupid enough to do it all on my own." He understood. This is still an act of domestic violence even though he didn't harm her. His girlfriend could become extremely fearful for her own well-being to think that if he could do that to a wall, he could do that to her some other time.

 Others may be more inclined to blame the other person: "Look what you made me do!" I still cringe when I hear a parent say to their child, "Don't make me (do this or that)." No child or another person ever made anyone do what they choose to do. Our behavior is always a choice.

If another person, who is of no importance to you in your life, behaves in a way in which you disapprove, why would you want to give that person control over how you choose to feel? Simply don't react. You have no need to get involved in verbal barbs, insults, or threats with someone who is not a part of your life. It takes two or more people to argue or fight. Let it be. When did you ever win an argument by successfully getting someone to believe what you do?

If someone important to you is not behaving the way you want them to behave, change what you want and/or change how you behave when you don't get what you want. If the problem is one of importance, deal with it by utilizing the seven caring habits. Will what you are about to say or do bring you closer together or will it drive you apart? You are the only person you can blame for your anger because it is a choice. You can always choose to be calm, respectful, negotiate, and listen to each other in ways that will bring you together in your disagreements instead of harming your relationship. How many times has your anger ever resulted in your preferred results? How many times has your anger harmed your relationship and perhaps even resulted it its demise?

Chapter 12 - Go Sell Crazy Someplace Else

One of the major roadblocks facing the improvement of "Mental Health" is the medical/psychiatric community, the media, and the general public's misunderstanding of just what mental health is. When I ask my group members or non-Choice Theory based audiences to come up with words depicting Mental Health, they invariably give me words that describe Mental Illness and not Mental Health. How can mental health be improved if it cannot be correctly identified?

A recent article posted on AOL boldly announced that the death of someone close to a person can "trigger mental disorders." What we have come to realize, and the world has yet to accept, is that the majority of what is being called "Mental Illness" is no more than unhappiness. . . and that any *long-term* unhappiness is the result of not having a satisfying relationship with the important people in one's life. Rather than reporting that certain events can trigger mental disorders, it would be more correctly stated that certain events can trigger "unhappiness." A person who is unhappy may not be as mentally healthy as they could be but they are not mentally ill.

Is there really such a thing as mental illness? . . . absolutely. Alzheimer's, Parkinson's, Mental Retardation, and Tourette's, are just some examples of mental illnesses. These are brain disorders that have pathology. However, one would not see a General Practitioner or psychiatrist to treat them. They would seek the help of a neurologist. So now, according to some professional individuals, should someone close to you die and you grieve their loss, you are now considered to be mentally disordered.

Declaring *unhappiness* as the source of aberrant behavior would be too naïve a concept for the world to accept. Rather than accept a person's unhappiness as the real cause of what appears to be a mental illness, the general consensus is that a patho-physiological condition exists and that it is the cause of one's behavior. "Normal people don't behave like that. It must be a mental disease!" This tenet is strongly held even when no patho-physiological conditions exist and with absolutely no laboratory tests to prove that they do exist.

A person who has been living in frustration and unhappiness for a long period of time is not experiencing the relationship that they would like to have with the important person(s) in their life. They try many things to make the relationship better so they can feel better. But when nothing they have done has been successful, they create behaviors that best serves the purpose to ease their unhappiness and frustration at the time.

After a long while, they may eventually give up on focusing on the relationship, disconnect from others, and begin to focus only on easing their frustration and unhappiness. It is these behaviors that others see as being odd, strange, weird, and mentally ill. Observers fail to see that these behaviors are meant to ease their unhappiness at that particular moment that they perform them. While it may look like mental illness to you, it seems the most appropriate thing for the unhappy person to do at the time they do it. Why? Because everything else they have tried hasn't worked. They would feel even more frustrated if they didn't have these behaviors to rely on to acquire some modicum of relief from their unhappiness.

Why do some people choose such things as schizophrenic type behaviors over other behaviors such as Obsessive Compulsive behaviors, or depression, anxiety, or ADD/ADHD, Bipolarism or resorting to murder? Because it's whatever they discovered to do first that had any effect of easing their unhappiness and frustration.

Have you ever been so frustrated and unhappy that you felt like you were going to "lose control?" This is what it is like for those who feel the way you have. Only they have been fighting it for longer periods than you may have. It is not a mental illness. It is an emotional condition. They are not as mentally healthy as they could be but they are not mentally ill. They are often quite "normal" during times when they are not so frustrated.

Their behavior is the result of an emotional condition resulting from their particular situation and not a physical/medical condition or illness. Fortunately, most people choose to depress before relying on the extreme measure of murdering others.

The act of mass shooting is the result of choosing something to do when everything else they have tried to do to ease their frustration and unhappiness has failed.

There is no conclusive, scientific evidence provided in the American Psychiatric Association's (APA's) bible, the "Diagnostic and Statistical Manual for Mental Disorders" (DSM) that is relied upon to diagnose mental illness. The creators and writers of this book openly admit under the heading of "<u>Associated Laboratory Findings</u>: *There are no laboratory tests that have been established as diagnostic in the assessment of schizophrenia, bipolar, Anxiety, ADD/ADHD*" or any of the other 400 listed mental illnesses in the DSM.

Would a dentist perform a root canal or extraction without first looking at X-rays to justify the existence of a condition that would warrant such a procedure? Would a doctor start chemotherapy or insulin treatment without the proof that a patient had a pathological condition and laboratory tests that indicate this treatment be conducted?

Yet unhappy people, who are severely frustrated as a result of not finding a way to satisfy the relationships with the important people in their life, are being diagnosed by general practitioners and psychiatrists with diseases they don't have and with medications that have no curative abilities and can, in some cases, lead to aggressive and suicidal behavior. Psych medications are harming the brain by keeping it from functioning the way it is normally supposed to function.

Today, many of the mass shooters we have come to experience are commonly unhappy people and being labeled "mentally ill." They are young men generally between the ages of fifteen and twenty-five, who are, or were, on psychotropic medications. They are shooting people in schools, airports, military bases, and shopping centers. There are occasional instances where the shooter is older but even then, in each case, they were having relationship problems with the important people in their lives and feeling unable to overcome their unhappiness.

If mass murder is a mental illness, why are these shooters only men and none of them women? If mentally ill, why are most shooters under the age of twenty-six? These are the questions that need to be addressed. If mental illness is the cause, then where is the pathology? Where are the lab tests to prove a disease exists? Is mental illness gender specific only to males below the age of twenty-six? These questions are not being answered because the focus is being placed in all the wrong areas. All of these mass murder shooters have these things in common and therefore very important to consider.

Instead, the only common traits that are being considered are: "They all had guns and shot lots of people. Therefore, they must be mentally ill and we don't know what to do except put them on psych meds and blame the NRA and the mental health community." The most recent mass-shooting incident took place in Las Vegas. The shooter's autopsy concluded that he no brain abnormality. Even if he did, there is no lab test to prove mental illness. The majority of those who have been diagnosed as mentally ill are not violent people who commit murder.

What is factual is that the National Institute of Mental Health (NIMH), the American Psychiatric Association (APA), and any medical group or organization that exists today, cannot provide scientific evidence that a psychiatric disorder or illness is the result of an objective and confirmable brain abnormality. Mental Illness is being diagnosed by decree and not by physical evidence. And this is why Mental Health cannot be improved until it can first be accurately identified and defined.

Solutions:

1. Stop calling mood disorders mental illnesses with a physical cause.

2. Make mental health a public health issue and not a medical health issue and stop treating it as a medical condition. Treating a non-medical condition by means of medical procedures has never worked and will not work other than to harm the patient.

3. Educate unhappy and currently happy people how to resolve their unhappiness and frustration with the important people in their lives . . . their mothers, fathers, siblings, personal relationships, with themselves, an employer, and perhaps a teacher.

4. Teach our children how to resolve conflict and get along well with others . . . something that has been missing since the beginning of mankind.

5. Focus on teaching in schools the things students need to know and can use in their life and not things they will never need to use or know or even want to know.

Mental Health has one major drawback . . . There's no money in it. There is only money in Mental Illness.

Most of the screening tools used for mental health assessments and diagnoses are created by those who will profit from the results.

There are many places people can go to improve and maintain their physical health, i.e. gyms, spas, fitness clubs, and even schools have physical education programs for exercise and health. Where does one go to improve or maintain their mental health?

If you suggested a mental health clinic, the odds are that you would be diagnosed with a mental illness. If you don't present with any mental illness symptoms, they have no way of knowing how to improve your mental health. There are no mental health gyms, fitness clubs, spas, or mental education programs. So if you are unhappy, like so many millions of people, your only choice is to go where they treat mental illness and you will be prescribed medications that affect your brain's normal ability to function and quite possibly told that you must stay on these medications because there is nothing anything or anyone else can do for you for the rest of your life.

The DSM V is the labeling bible used by most everyone in the psychiatric community of counselors, therapists, psychologists, and psychiatrists.

Dr. Glasser considered the DSM as "The most dangerous book ever written."

Today, the common form of treatment used by psychiatrists is to prescribe medication and no counseling. The general approach utilized by counselors, therapists, and psychologists are to diagnose using the DSM V and then referring clients to psychiatrists or general medical practitioners for medication. There may also be talk therapy offered by the counselors or therapists along with possible medication.

Now let's compare the process of when you see your medical doctor as opposed to a mental health practitioner. When you see your doctor for physical illness, the medical agency looks for symptoms and pathology to support the diagnosis. If no pathology exists, they don't usually medicate or treat something that they can't find. The key word here is "usually." Fibromyalgia has no pathology but several doctors are treating it with opiate pain medication. Many patients complaining of pain have no discovered pathology and opiate drugs are being prescribed like Pez dispensers. This is a leading cause of opiate addiction that has become a national epidemic.

I have written previously that Dr. Glasser states that the most common way people express their unhappiness is through aches and pains. When someone goes to their doctor concerning pain and the doctor cannot find any cause or reason for the pain, they will often prescribe addictive opiate medication anyway. Pain is also the most common reason clients give doctors so that they can be prescribed medical marijuana.

When I interview all of my clients, I always inquire about their physical and mental health and any medications they are taking. When I discover a client who reports he has a medical marijuana card, I ask them for what cause was the prescription made. Ninety percent will tell me it is for pain from a fall or car wreck years ago, or a sports injury that plagues them even though their doctor can't find anything wrong with them. Those who deny any pain but still acquired a medical marijuana card say they got it, "So I can smoke weed legally." But I digress.

The methods relied upon to diagnose physical illness are not put into practice when it comes to mental illness. The DSM may correctly identify behaviors but it openly admits there are no laboratory tests or other objective tests to indicate the existence of any brain abnormality or illness. The diagnoses are made only by symptoms and no supportive pathology. In other words, it is medical science by decree. "You look and behave like you have a mental illness so we are going to put you on psychiatric medication."

How many patients would willingly take insulin or chemotherapy treatment if there were no lab tests or pathology to support the diagnosis of diabetes or cancer? Rather than relying on pathology to determine mental illness, the DSM was created by a group of individuals who decided by consensus or agreement what should be declared or diagnosed as a mental illness.

Dr. Thomas S. Szasz, M.D. wrote, *"It is important to understand clearly that modern psychiatry and the identification of new psychiatric diseases, began not by indentifying such diseases by means of the established methods of pathology, but by creating a new criterion of what constitutes disease . . . thus, whereas in modern medicine new diseases were discovered, in modern psychiatry they were invented."*[3]

---

[3] Szasz, Thomas S., (1974) "The Myth of Mental Illness: Foundations of a Theory of Personal Conduct," (Revised Edition), Harper & Row Publishers.

In her book "Psyched Out," author Kelly Patricia O'Meara
writes:

> *"There is no known objective, confirmable abnormality
> of the brain for depression, schizophrenia, obsessive-
> compulsive disorder or bipolar disorder. These mental
> disorders like all the other alleged psychiatric mental
> disorders are determined by the "experts" in mental
> health based on agreement of subjective criteria . . .
> lists of behavioral symptoms that essentially are
> opinions."[4]*

As long as the medical model is used in mental health
applications, there will always be a disparity between Mental
Health and Mental Illness. What will continue to keep these
two concepts apart will not be medical science or
consensus. It will be power and money.

The drug companies will continue to make up diseases and
medications for illnesses that don't exist that result in billions
of dollars in sales. Counselors and Therapists will continue
to refer clients to psychiatrists and General Practitioners for
medication because it makes their prestigious career seem

---

[4] O'Meara, Kelly Patricia, "Psyched Out." Author House, Bloomington, IN, p.31

as important as that as a medical doctor. Lobbyists will continue to lobby for more and more laws pertaining to mental illness and programs for the sake of drug utilizing agencies that will prescribe medication. Talk therapy and counseling techniques are now removed from college and university syllabi and replaced with pharmacology courses. Today's psychiatrists are not trained in the art and technique of talk therapy.

Television ads and misinformation about what causes "mental Illness" are being fed to the world's viewing audience all for the sake of selling drugs. Have you noticed that with all of the television ads for medication, the only medications for mental illness are for depression? Where are the medical ads for anxiety, schizophrenia, bipolar, and obsessive-compulsive disorders? Doctors are prescribing them. Why aren't they televised? It seems that depression is so commonplace that it is an acceptable condition to have. But the pharmaceutical companies don't know how to depict someone in a commercial that could depict someone with schizophrenia, anxiety, bipolar, or obsessive-compulsive behaviors in an acceptable light without outrage from those who have been given such a label and from the general public.   The irony is, it would appear that such diagnoses are considered a character disorder more than a medical condition. Yet the general public and professionals would still opt for them to be but on psych meds. This exemplifies the power and belief in the medical model of treating behavior.

Madman vs Happyman

What would you say is the opposite of the word, "Madman?" Happyman? The word Madman was used in the reporting yet another mass shooting spree . . . this one by twenty-two year old mass shooter, Elliot Rodger. Ironically, the use of the word "Madman" is as close as society will come to the real cause of Elliot's choice to kill 6 people and wound several more. This is because the use of the word, "Madman," is perceived as being Mad as in "Insane," "Crazy," or "Daft." Yet, if asked what the opposite of "Mad" is, they would most likely say, "Happy." So why isn't the opposite of Madman a Happyman? Shouldn't the goal of mental health be to help transition one's mental illness of a madman towards that of a happy man?

Elliot and **many** of the other mass shooters over the last few years were all unhappy and "detached" young men under the age of twenty-five and all who had been on, or were currently on, psych meds. Yet the world will not accept that unhappiness is why these young men attempt to ease their frustration and anger. Incidentally, why aren't any of these mass shooters women? Does this form of so-called "mental illness" only affect the male gender?

People don't go around shooting other people because they are happy. Why don't we start right there? People shoot other people because they are unhappy. Why are all of these young men unhappy? ...because they are not experiencing satisfying relationships with the important people in their lives. It hasn't anything to do with some past traumatic event several years ago or some pathology that doesn't exist. It is an unhappy situation that is going on in the present at that moment in their life. Their unhappiness lies within a very unsatisfying relationship with such possible persons as a mother, a father, a sibling, a boy or girlfriend, a husband/wife, an employer, possibly a teacher, or even an unsatisfying relationship with themselves.

When a person has exhausted all that they have tried to do to resolve their unhappiness by trying to control what they cannot control, they often detach from friends, family, and even society. They may believe that people don't like them so why should they like people? Since they don't like people, it means nothing to them to exact revenge for their anger on people they may or may not even know.

If they have been, or currently are on psych meds . . .these medications drug the mind with no curative powers but shut off the brains ability to be creative to resolve their unhappiness in more logical and appropriate ways. Seeking ways to resolve intense distress, they rationalize with a drugged mind, that eliminating specific people, or people in general, will ease their frustration. Psychotropic medications are no more than what Dr. Peter Breggin calls "chemical lobotomies." They are not selective in the emotions that drug companies report target specifically.

If a drug has an effect on one emotion, it has an effect on all emotions. Elliot Roger was receiving "professional help" according to the family's attorney. The report was that after his parents notified others about their son's you tube post, *Police interviewed Elliot Rodger and found him to be a "perfectly polite, kind and wonderful human," he added. Police did not find a history of guns, but did say Rodger "didn't have a lot of friends," had trouble making friends, and didn't have any girlfriends.*

They failed to recognize any condition because they were looking for signs of "a madman." While Elliot was mad, others were looking for "craziness." People who have mental illness don't turn their illness off and on when they feel like it. Anyone is capable of changing his or her thoughts and subsequent emotions at any given time.

If being interviewed for possible signs of insanity or criminal activity, a person can easily think and emote naturally. What the police failed to recognize as the cause of his behavior is his relationship unhappiness, even when they admitted he had relationship problems with others. They simply glide right over the source and cause and look for other signs of what they believe to be mental illness.

Until the world begins to address the real cause of what is being called mental illness, nothing will change. What is being called mental illness is the behavior of unhappy people who are having difficulty with the important people in their lives. While not everyone who is unhappy resorts to mass shootings, others have found other creative ways or behavior to ease their frustration.

These behaviors are identified by decree of the psychiatric delivery system as:

- Schizophrenia
- Severe anxiety
- Obsessive-compulsive behavior
- Depression
- Bipolar
- ADD/ADHD
- And any other mental illness listed in the DSM. While the symptomatic behaviors of these conditions are accurate, they have no medical or physical, or organic, or genetic pathology. These behaviors serve

to ease one's frustration and anger regarding his/her unhappiness that is rooted in unsatisfying relationships. Mental Health will not improve until the focus is placed on the true source of the behavior . . . unhappiness.

If you don't change your beliefs, your life will be like this forever. Is that good news?
- W. Somerset Maugham

What we have been doing in psychiatry for the last hundred years has been half-baked.
- William Glasser, MD

Dr. G.L. Harrington, a mentor of Dr. Glasser, has stated: *"If all the professionals in our field suddenly disappeared, the world would hardly note their absence."* His reference being that if there were no psychiatric professionals, there would not be any change in the amount of unhappy people who exist in the world.

For over a century, psychiatry has been focusing on and teaching those in the psychiatric community that mental illness is a medical condition. As a result, the majority of the world believes this to be true. This is why the psychiatric communities' efforts in dealing with mental health have not been effective.

Unhappiness is not a medical condition nor is it chemical imbalances in one's brain that the pharmaceutical companies would have you believe. There is no physical pathology to what is being called mental illness. With no pathology, there is no medical or physical cause.

Doctors and psychiatrists have been treating people for diseases that don't exist with medications that have no chance of remedying something that has no pathology. The only thing these drugs do is drug a person's brain, numb their emotions, and have a history of causing many to commit suicide or do harm to others. . . sometimes both at the same time.

The medical profession refuses to consider unhappy relationships as the cause of "mental Illness" because it doesn't fit into their medical mind-set. To them, anything that is not medical is not worth considering. So they claim mental illness to be a medical condition. It is science by decree. This is why mental illness and mental health are not improving.

Until just recently, you could not find a definition of Mental Health anywhere in any dictionary or any clinical publication until Dr. Glasser gave his definition:

> *You are mentally healthy if you enjoy being with most of the people you know, especially with the important people in our life such as family, sexual partners and friends. Generally, you are happy and are more than willing to help an unhappy family member, friend, or colleague to feel better. You lead a mostly tension-free life, laugh a lot, and rarely suffer from the aches and pains that so many people accept as an unavoidable part of living.*

> *You enjoy life and have no trouble accepting other people who think and act differently from you. It rarely occurs to you to criticize or try to change anyone. If you have differences with someone else you will try to work out the problem; if you can't you will walk away before you argue and increase the difficulty.*

> *You are creative in what you attempt and may enjoy more of your potential than you ever thought possible. Finally, even in very difficult situations when you are unhappy – no one can be happy all of the*

It wasn't until Dr. Glasser wrote his definition that anyone could find a definition of "Mental Health." At best it could only be defined as "the absence of mental illness," in any and all dictionaries.

Since then The World Health Organization (WHO) and several other sources have announced a watered-down version of Dr. Glasser's definition including the Merriam-Webster Dictionary that previously had nothing listed. Now you can find several versions of Dr. Glasser's definition.

What it particularly interesting, including that of the Mayo Clinic's definition, is that <u>none of the definitions cite a medical condition as the cause or source of any mental illness.</u> So why is it being treated unsuccessfully with medications and techniques that have no medical or physical causes?

A person's symptoms of what is being called metal illness can always be found in their unhappiness. Someone important to them, or some important situation in their life, is not the way they want them, or the situation, to be. The image of what they want in their Quality World and what they have do not match. They have been trying to control something they can't control and out of total frustration, have resorted to behaviors that are seen and diagnosed as mental illnesses. While these behaviors do not necessarily offer solutions to their unhappiness, they do provide easement to their frustration.

People don't go around shooting other people because they are happy. Nor do they have a chemical imbalance in their brains that make them do such things . . . unless it is an imbalance created by the medications they have been given.

When a person has tried everything they know how and what to do to ease their frustration from unsatisfying relationships, they grasp at any behavior that comes to mind that they haven't utilized so far. These behaviors take the form of what is being called "Mental Illness." If the behavior has even the slightest effect of easing their frustration, they rely on it. To not do so would only cause them to feel more unhappy than if they are if they didn't do them. When they choose unconventional behavior, it makes perfectly good sense to them at the moment.

Why won't we see this changing anytime soon?   The survival of the pharmaceutical companies and the psychiatric profession appears to be more important to the powers that be than the consideration of society's well being.

There is currently a world-wide group of professionals who are speaking out on social media, lecturing at conferences and universities, and organizing to inform the world of the myths, fallacies, and lies of psychiatry.

Additional Mental Health improvement measures:

- Make Mental Health a Public Health Issue just as Physical Health has done.
- Educate the public that mental illness is not a medical condition and stop treating it as such.
- Cease the use of psychotropic medications except in such cases where harm to others may exist.
- Take the medical model out of psychiatry and drop the diagnosis.
- Teach people how to improve their relationships and get along with others.
- Teach people how to take responsibility for their own happiness and not to blame others for their lack of it.
- Teach people all the things they do to control others when the only people they can control is themselves.

- Teaching people what is missing in their lives that are keeping them from their happiness and to discovering ways to get these needs met without infringing on the needs and rights of others.

In other words: Teach the world Choice Theory.

As of **this date** the William Glasser Institute has trained 92,360 people with continued new trainees every few months around the world.

So far, over 12,136 individuals are certified in Choice Theory and Reality Therapy and this figure changes every few months.

All human beings, regardless of race, religion, or culture, behave from the moment of our birth until death. The purpose of any behavior are choices we make in our efforts to satisfy any one or more of our five basic and genetic needs for **Survival; Love and Belonging**; the **Power** of Acceptance, Appreciation, Respect, Achievement, and Control (Positive or negative); **Freedom** to come and go as we please and make our own decisions; and **Fun** in the form of learning and recreating.

We have amassed many behaviors to satisfy these happiness needs from what we have learned from parents, teachers, and from our personal experiences of what worked for us. We also invented some behaviors when all else we knew to meet our happiness wants and needs.

Whenever we perceive something outside ourselves (external perceptions) that doesn't meet our (internal) personal images of what we want, believe, and value . . . it tends to be human nature to take measures to control what is perceived externally to match what is wanted, believed, or valued internally.

Whatever it is that we want to control will serve to satisfy one or more of our five basic needs. What leads to frustration and unhappiness is trying to control people and things that we cannot control.

Over the years, and due to my knowledge of Choice Theory, I have kept from choosing to depress or anger on any and all things that life throws at me. I realize that I have a choice on how to perceive the situation and I can see it as sad, fearful, or indifferent. The first thing I do when faced with an unhappy situation is to ascertain if the situation is something that I can control or not. I know that I can only control myself. If there is something positive and internally controllable that I can do to remedy a situation, then I do it. If I have a flat tire, I have options to control it. I can fix it myself or call my insurance company who will provide roadside service. I can't imagine anyone being pleased that they have a flat tire. The discovery of such is not a good thought that elicits happy feelings. I can choose to be as upset, disappointed, and angry as I want but none of those emotions are going to remedy the problem. I'm ultimately going to have to have the tire fixed or replaced with a spare so why get all upset over something that has to be done anyway? So I have my first reaction of "Damn! Just what I don't want." Then accept the reality of the situation and save myself the aggravation and unhappiness by doing whatever is necessary to get back to the state of mind that I want. Continuing to swear and get upset while taking care of the situation would only continue to feed and augment unwanted thoughts and emotions that could get in the way of finding a resolution to the problem. I have a choice on my thoughts and emotions regarding my situation.

But if I am having a problem with another person, I don't call "Clamenza" to "take care of it." Nor do I choose to look at other options that I can do to get even or coerce the other person to change.

The key here, when in conflict with others, is "Acceptance." It is what it is. Other people are who and what they are and accept that fact. Acceptance does not mean agreeing with them. It means you accept that this is how they are or this is their particular position and you are not about to be able to change them.

When it comes to differences of opinion, you may highly disagree with someone but know that no amount of arguing or debate will ever cause them to change their position. So why even bother? How many times have you gotten in a heated discussion with someone and you walked away having transformed their thinking? I would venture to guess you had no success in doing so. This is where Paul

McCartney's mother Mary would tell him, "Let It Be" comes into play. It is what it is so move on knowing there's nothing you can do about it.

If you have been absorbing the Choice Theory components of which I have been writing, you might be thinking to yourself, "Hey, Choice Theory guy! Isn't what you are doing by writing this book essentially telling us what is right for us because it is right for you? " You got me. In one sense, the answer is a definite "Yes." However, the purpose behind this book is not to control you. You still have the choice to see its benefits and have a positive effect on your life if you apply it or simply disregard any or all of it and keep on doing what you're doing and continuing to keep on getting what you're getting. The choice is yours and it is not my place to convince you or coerce you otherwise.

All I am doing in this book is offering you information and information does not "make" you behave. It only gives you the opportunity to choose what to do with the information. You may get the information that someone wants to talk to you on the phone when it rings but the ringing phone did not "make" you answer it. You choose to either answer it or refuse to accept the call. I will sleep well tonight whether or not you find this information to be advantageous or if you choose to see it as a lot of bunk and baloney. And that is Choice Theory.

Choice Theory teaches us that if things are not the way we want them to be, we have specific behaviors we can choose that will effectively satisfy, or at least ease, our frustration and unhappiness.

1. The knowledge that the only person we can control is our self.

2. The knowledge that trying to control something that cannot be controlled is a waste of time and effort, leads to anger and frustration, and likely lead to making poor choices that will make the situation worse. Let it be.

3. The knowledge that if you try to control another person you will cause harm to the relationship and distance you from each other rather than bringing you closer. Let it be.

4. The knowledge that what may be right for you may not always be right for anyone else. Live your life in the way it works for you and let others live their life the way they choose. Live and let live.

5. Not everyone that we encounter in our life will be happy people all or most of the time. We all have our bad days once in awhile. Other people's behavior towards you while striving for happiness has more to do with them than it does you. They are not getting one or more of their basic needs of happiness met and they are struggling to take control to get those needs met . . . even if they perceive you as part of their problem.

You may not know what it is that they perceive but whatever it is, is the reason for their behavior and their effort to find happiness and resolution. Some individuals struggle for long periods of time . . . even a lifetime. They are not only toxic to themselves, but toxic to you as well. They are a threat towards maintaining your own happiness. They have yet to learn how to effectively deal with their own unhappiness and many of the behaviors they created have only been slightly less frustrating. This is why they continue to use them and not discover more effective ways to deal with their unhappiness. To them, a little bit of happiness is better than no happiness. They develop some tolerance and become somewhat comfortable in an uncomfortable situation.

Keep your distance and be understanding or, if necessary, divorce yourself from them. Accept their behavior for who and what they are for reasons you are not aware of other than they are doing the only thing they know to do at the time to get their needs met. Don't allow the toxic behavior of unhappy people to destroy your own happiness and well-being.

6. Above it all, the two most important ways to find and maintain your own happiness when things aren't going your way are:

   a. **Change what you want**.

   b. **Change how you behave when you don't get
      what you want.**

It doesn't get any easier or simpler than that. Want proof? Recall the last time you were very upset and unhappy over any given period of time and now, today, the situation is of no concern.

Whatever the situation was at the time is not an issue today because you overcame it… without realizing how you did it. What you did was change the way you wanted things to be and you stopped whatever it was that you had been doing to deal with it. You found happiness.

Most importantly, for your own sake as well as anyone in which you are in conflict, is understanding that they are only doing what they can with the lack of knowledge and skills to resolves their unhappiness without controlling you. Their intent is to get one or more of their basic needs met and they are relying on harmful external control methods to get you to do or believe something that you aren't doing. You can't change them or teach them as long as they are being difficult. Even if you were to explain a better way for them to approach the situation, they may not likely be willing to do so even if they knew it would help. They are in their defensive mode and not willing to let their guard down. You just aren't behaving the way they want you to. Instead of coming together, they are pushing you away from them. This will not cause a resolution to your differences.

Likewise, don't get caught up in the controlling battle when someone utilizes the seven distancing habits on you. It is so very common that when one person begins using the controlling behaviors that the person on the receiving end begins to fire back controlling behaviors of their own. Two people trying to control each other's beliefs or behaviors will both end up losers. Walk away from the argument or simply change the subject after agreeing to disagree. If someone not important to you in your life has a problem with you, then who has the problem? Don't let someone else's problem

become your problem. Walk away and let them be as upset
and   as   unhappy   as   they   choose   to   be.

Chapter 13 – Regrets

Some of you may know, while others have yet to learn . . . life goes by in a blink. And the older one may get, the faster the blinks occur.

As we look back on our life, we realize that things didn't always turn out the way we wished they had. But be assured . . . the way things turned out was not always a bad thing. Sure, we all have regrets and some that we don't even remember until we reach the September of our years. But whatever happened has happened. No matter how much you may wish they had turned out differently, the fact remains . . . we cannot change the past and whatever happened, happened.

As one who has had more regrets than I previously realized until I began to review my life, I can truthfully tell you that life is truly what we make it. We have all made choices in our pursuit to attain happiness and some of those choices didn't work out too well for us. These choices we made, both effective and ineffective, pertain to all of us. Each of us has had our share of good and poor choices. The manner is which we reacted to these choices, at the time, determined our happiness or sadness.

I'm reminded of the Paul Anka lyric: "Regrets, I've had a few, but then again, too few to mention." Actually, I contend that we have more than a few regrets . . . that we are willing to admit. This is not necessarily a bad thing. We don't want to feel miserable about things that happened in the past or things we did, especially if we feel we made bad choices or if others treated us wrongfully. Some of our regrets are purposely repressed.

Some of the things we may have done in the past are things we may not have considered to be wrong at the time. It's often when we look back over our life that we recall some of our past behaviors and suddenly realize that we were wrong in our actions.

While forgiving others for any wrong doings perpetrated on us, we also will need to forgive ourselves for our own past errors in judgment. We are all human which means we are in no way perfect. We are prone to make mistakes and bad choices. We were only doing the best we could at the time with limited information and poor resolution skills. We may have done wrong but as long as we feel remorseful about our choices, we earn the right to be forgiven.

It's difficult for one to choose sadness when we know we have a choice on how we want to feel. Choice Theory allows us the freedom to release us from our regrets. It is all done by virtue of one word: Acceptance.

Whatever happened has happened and nothing we can say or do can ever change it. It is what it is. It may be regretful but the fact remains . . . it happened and it was real. When you acknowledge this, you have reached the first step of Acceptance.

Now you have a choice of how you will react to the reality of the past regret. Whatever may have happened to you and whatever you may have done to someone else involved the element of one who was trying to satisfy one or more of the basic needs of Survival, Love and Belonging, Power, Freedom, and Fun.

Whatever happened was their, or your, best attempt at the time to get these needs met. You can choose to dwell on the past and feel miserable and not be willing to accept the past chosen behavior of others, feel guilty about your own past chosen behavior, or forgive them and/or yourself for the choices either of you may made at the time.

You can choose to understand that the behavior of others is how they choose to deal with their unhappiness or you can choose to be miserable about whatever that they do and carry it around with you forever, to your unhappy heart's content.

The next step is the choice to forgive . . . either yourself or someone whom you may feel has wronged you in the past. Forgiveness is a choice. The concept of forgiveness is to forgive others for your sake, not so much theirs. Forgiving them in your mind takes away your anger and unhappiness. When I hear a client tell me that they just can't forgive someone for something another person has done, I remind them that they can forgive them but they just don't want to forgive them. I ask them how long do they want to hold resentments toward another person when the other person may not care any less whether they forgive them or not? I ask them to describe their anger and resentment to me and then ask them how it affects them physically and emotionally. Then I ask them if they enjoy feeling as miserable as they describe it to be. I explain that it is practically impossible to choose to be miserable and unhappy when you know you have a choice.

Forgiveness does not mean to forget unless the transgression is trivial or minor. In such cases, it is a simple choice to both forgive and not hold grudges. When seriously wronged by someone, it is possible to forgive him or her but not forget. Forgiveness allows you to free yourself from allowing the other person to have an emotional control over you.

It is often easier for some people to forgive another person for any transgression than it is to forgive one's self for any transgression that they may have performed. To not feel any remorse of having made a poor choice that may have affected another person only connotes one who has no respect or empathy for anyone including him/herself.

Feeling remorseful for any past indiscretion is necessary for the elements of Acceptance and Forgiveness of one's self as well as for anyone who may have transgressed against us. But even remorse can be taken too far. Beating one's self up mentally and emotionally will do little to allow one to move forward towards their happiness.

Accept the reality of any loss or transgression, grieve a little bit, forgive yourself and/or others, and move on with your life. Change what you want. Change how you behave when you don't get what you want. Do both if it is applicable.

Putting It All Into Play

You're not crazy. You're not mentally ill. You're unhappy. You're unhappy because things or are not the way you want them to be and/or you don't have the relationship that you would like to have with someone important to you. It might even be a bad relationship with yourself.

Using the two-column assessment of the Basic Needs, which of them indicate a gap of 2 or more from what you want and what you have? If more than one Basic Need is lacking, put them in order as to their importance to you.

An example might be that your Love and Belonging needs, Power Needs, and Fun Needs may be lacking. If so, then place each of the needs in descending order with the first one being the most important.

What do you want or how do you want things to be?

Accepting the fact and knowing that the only person you can control is yourself and/or that what you want is something either you can or cannot control, what have you been doing to get what you want or to get the relationship that you desire?

How effective have your efforts to get your need(s) met? How many of these behaviors do you continue to utilize even though they don't return the results you want? Stop any and all actions that have no beneficial effect in satisfying your wants.

When dealing with another person, how many of the Seven Distancing Behaviors of Criticizing, Blaming, Complaining, Nagging, Punishing, Threatening, or Bribing to control have you been doing? Immediately stop any and all of them. Whether or not you replace them with the Seven Caring Habits at once is not as important as to stop using the distancing behaviors once and for all when dealing with others.

You cannot change another person. Their behavior choices serve the same purpose that yours serve . . . to meet one or more of your basic needs. They are going about it the best way they know how as you are doing as well. The same needs . . . just different ways to satisfy them. Either accept them as they are or move on. Sometimes, those who are the closest to us are those who are the most toxic to us. They can't make you angry or even happy. Any emotions you experience are internally created and the result of external stimuli. You always have a choice on how to think and act which allows you the luxury of allowing pleasant emotions and a sense of physical well-being.

What have you not done to satisfy your Basic Needs that may be lacking? Use your creativity and come up with several different things you could do that you haven't done yet. Be sure that whatever you create is something that is legal, ethical, and will not impose or harm the Basic Needs of someone else, even if they are not part of your concern. If something doesn't result in your happiness, then try something else.

Two things you can do right now that won't take much effort is to accept the reality of your situation, accept it for what it is, and:

1. Change what you want.

2. Change how you behave when you aren't getting what you want.

In many cases, your unhappiness will end right then and there.

Take responsibility for your own life. Stop blaming others for your unhappiness. Climb out of any victim role you may have created over the years. You're situation may involve someone else or other people but you are the only person who can manage to rise above any adversity. You can't change whatever may have happened in the near or far past, but you can control how you deal with now and tomorrow.

Don't wait for others to come running to your aid or doing things for you that you could very well do for yourself. Likewise, don't get caught up in the muck and mire of other people's unhappiness by doing for them the things they could do for themselves.

When in conflict with another person whom you consider to be an important person in your life, use your creativity to come up with some behaviors or things you can do for the sake of your relationship with them.

When in conflict with others, there are three entities involved:

1. You.
2. The other person.
3. And the relationship.

What can you do for the sake of the relationship and not something that you can do for the other person.

You can only do what you can do. Don't try to be all things to all people. Be the person you are, naturally, without trying to live up to the expectations or wants of others. If you can't accept yourself, you will have a hard time accepting anyone else. For all things that you cannot control, whatever the situation that is out of your hands . . . Let It Be. As Paul McCartney reminds us, "There will be an answer . . . Let it be, let it be."

Forgive yourself for any past sins of omission or commission. We are all prone to make mistakes and poor choices in our lives. It's all part of being human. Our errors were the best choices we had at the time to satisfy any one or more of our Basic Needs. Admit your errors and wherever possible, make amends with those whom you may have wronged . . . as long as it doesn't lead to the other person taking action against you or if your admission of wrongdoing doesn't harm or involve others associated with the person with whom you make amends. Be advised that those with whom you attempt to make amends do not have to accept your apologies. If they do, then that is wonderful. But if they don't, that is okay as well. The important thing is that you did what you had to do for yourself and if they don't accept an apology or if they are unwilling to forgive, then who has the problem? Let it be.

Whenever you experience an anxiety attack, choose to depress, have difficulty concentrating, hear voices, acquire aches and pains that doctors can't identify with any pathology, or choose any number of other behaviors that others may consider strange or "crazy," there are always more satisfying choices you can make to resolve your unhappiness that don't require pharmaceuticals or addictive substances.

Patience and perseverance are required when applying all of the elements of Choice Theory. It won't all fall into place at once. It requires modifying the way you have been thinking and acting for several years and that in itself, is not an easy progression. But I can promise you this: You will find practically an immediate change in your life and your relationship with others when you eliminate any one or more of the Seven Distancing Behaviors. That's a good place to start. Read Dr. Glasser's other books on Choice Theory to fill in any spaces left open by this author's directives and vernacular.

Choice Theory. What a beautiful way to live.

About the Author

Michael Rice is a Licensed Independent Substance Abuse Counselor who is certified in Reality Therapy and Choice Theory by the William Glasser Institute. Mike has been in private practice since 1998 and over the years has helped over four thousand clients for substance abuse and several other behavioral health and emotional concerns. His years of practice and experience has encompassed group therapy, one-on-one, and couples counseling, helping others to better understand themselves by teaching Choice Theory methods of improving their relationships with the important people in their lives.

Mike has been an active member of the William Glasser Institute, having served as the Regional Director of the Western states as well as having served on the U.S. Board of Directors of the Institute. Mike has presented several workshops at conferences in AZ, CA, NV, TN, CT, and Bogota, Columbia. He has presented at the AZ Psychological Association and the Sierra Council on Alcoholism and Drug Dependence in Sacramento, CA. Along with Dr. Kenneth Larsen, Mike co-emceed the opening ceremonies of the William Glasser International Conference at Loyola Marymount University in Los Angeles in June of 2012.

Mike remains the CEO and Director of Court Counseling Services in Mesa, AZ, which he started in 1998. He continues to assess clients for substance abuse, teaches life-skills, and shares his experiences with client issues and Choice Theory applications in his books and articles.

References

For further reference information on the nature of current day psychology and psychiatry:

Glasser, Wm., M.D., *Warning: Psychiatry Can Be Dangerous To Your Mental Health*, New York, Harper Collins Publishers, Inc., 2003

Gosden, Richard, Ph.D. *Punishing the Patient: How Psychiatrists Misunderstand and Mistreat Schizophrenia.* Victoria, Australia: Scribe, 2001

Lynch, Terry, M.D. *Beyond Prozac: Healing Mental Health Suffering Without Drugs.* Dublin, Ireland: Merino Books, 2001

Breggin, Peter, M.D. *Toxic Psychiatry.* New York: St. Martin's Press, 1991

Breggin, Peter, M.D. and David Cohen, Ph.D. *Your Drug May Be Your Problem,* Reading , Mass.: Perseus Books, 1999.

Gosden, Richard, Ph,.D., *Punishing the Patient: How Psychiatrists Misunderstand and Mistreat Schizophrenia.* Victoria, Australia: Scibe, 2001

O'Meara, Kelly Patricia, *Psyched Out: How Psychiatry Sells Mental Illness and Pushes Pills That Kill.* Indiana and UK, Author House, 2006

Glasser, Wm. M.D. *Defining Mental Health as a Public Health Issue.(Pamphlet)* CA,WGlasser.com, 2005

Whitaker, Robert. *Mad in America: Bad Science, Bad Medicine, and the Enduring Mistreatment of the Mentally Ill.* Cambridge, MASS.: Perseus Publishing, 2002

Johnstone, Lucy. *Users and Abusers of Psychiatry,* 2nd Ed. London and Philadelphia: Routledge, 2000

Other books by Choice Theory authors:

Bellows, J. Thomas, Ph.D., *Happiness In The Family: Using Choice Theory To Eliminate Hostility In The Family,* iUniverse, 2007, Lincoln, NE.

Buck, Nancy S., Ph. D., *Peaceful Parenting*

Crawford, D, Bodine, R and Hoglund, R *The School for Quality Learning: Managing the School and Classroom the Deming Way,* Research Press, Champaign, IL 1994

McIntosh, Maureen Craig , *Choosing A Quality Loving Sexual Relationship: A Manual For Teachers, Counselors, & Parents Paperback– February 20, 2016*

Olver, Kim, MS, LCPC, Choosing Me: *Letting Go of What Doesn't Work and Making Room for What Does*

Olver, Kim, MS, LCPC, *Secrets of Happy Couples*

Walker, Doug. *The A-Ha Performance.*

Wubbolding, Robert, and John Brickell, *Counseling With Choice Theory.*

Wubbolding, Robert, Managing People

Wubbolding, Robert, *Reality Therapy for the 21st Century.*

Wubbolding, Robert, Reality Therapy: What Is It?

Wubbolding, Robert, Understanding Reality Therapy

Wubbolding, Robert, Using Reality Therapy

Web Sites

WGlasser.com

Mental Health and Happiness.com

http://www.wglasserbooks.com/

Facebook Pages:

Associations for Choice Theory - South Africa

Choice Theory Australia

Choice Theory Fan Club

Choice Theory in the Pacific, Africa and Asia PAACT

Choice Theory New Zealand

Choosing Excellence

Court Counseling Services

Drop The Disorder

European Institute for Reality Therapy

Mad In America

Peter R. Breggin, M.D.

Reality Therapy William Glasser International - Malaysia

Take Charge of Your Mind

William Glasser Institute Ireland

William Glasser Institute Philippines

William Glasser Institute Singapore

Other Books by Michael Rice

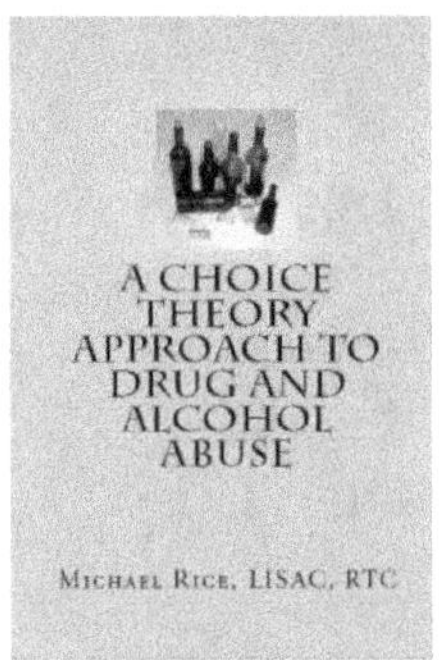

A Choice Theory Approach to Drug and   Alcohol Abuse
ISBN: 1449501079

For addicts/alcoholics, therapists/counselors, and anyone who lives with or loves an addicted person.

'Til Death Do Us Part, or 'Til You Piss Me Off, Whichever Comes First
ISBN: 1449503160
Why marriages and relationships fail and how to put them back together.

 Happiness is Just a Bowl of Choices
ISBN: 1449500897
Why people do the things they do which destroy what they want the most in life: Happiness. Learn ways to find and keep it.

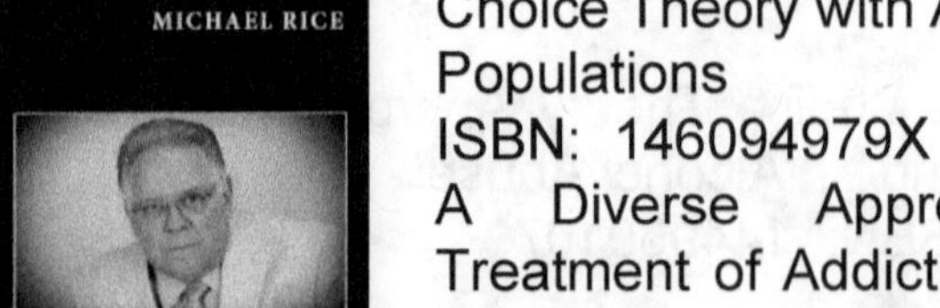

Choice Theory with Addicted Populations
ISBN: 146094979X
A Diverse Approach for the Treatment of Addictions. This book contains techniques, directives, ideas, and explanations for those who may be addicted to prescription meds, street drugs or alcohol

Leave Me Alone!
ISBN: 1497531861
Direct, blunt, and to the point designed for the reader to see the reality and truth of addiction. Directions and concepts are passed along to the reader to assist them on the road to a drug/alcohol-free life and newfound happiness.

Grow Old and Be Happy: A Work In Progress
This is a terrific book full of humor and good advice on how to cope with the aging process! A must read for seniors and anyone who is lucky enough to be one someday. Growing old is not a choice but staying happy as you age is.

9 781983 849930